Burpee Basics

perennials

Burpee Basics

perennials

A growing guide for easy, colorful gardens

Emma Sweeney

Macmillan • USA

MACMILLAN
A Simon & Schuster Macmillan Company
1633 Broadway
New York, NY 10019

MACMILLAN is a registered trademark of Macmillan, Inc.

BURPEE is a registered trademark of W. Atlee Burpee & Company

Library of Congress Cataloging-in-Publication Data

Sweeney, Emma.
  Perennials : a growing guide for easy, colorful gardens / by Emma Sweeney.
    p.   cm. — (Burpee basics)
  Includes index.
  ISBN: 0-02-862224-3 (alk. paper)
  1. Perennials.   I. Title.   II. Series.
  SB434.S94   1998
  635.9'32—dc21   98-38259
                                                         CIP

Manufactured in the United States of America

Book design by Nick Anderson

Line illustrations by Laura Robbins

Cover photograph by David Cavagnaro

Photography credits:
    W. Atlee Burpee Co.: pages 104, 109, 112, 114 (top), 116, 117 (top), 120, 121 (bottom), 122, 124 (top), 125, 126, 127, 128 (top), 130, 132, 134, 135, 136, 137, 138, 139, 147, 149 (bottom), 151, 152 (bottom), 156 (top), 158, 160, 162, 164 (bottom)
    Allen Rokeach, courtesy of W. Atlee Burpee Co.: pages 5, 43
    David Cavagnaro: pages ii, xiv, 26, 62, 90 (right), 100, 106, 107, 108, 110, 111, 114 (bottom), 115, 117 (bottom), 118, 119, 121 (top), 123, 124 (bottom), 128 (bottom), 129, 140, 141, 142, 144 (top), 145, 148, 149 (top), 150, 152 (top), 153, 156 (bottom), 157, 159, 161 (bottom), 163, 164 (top)
    Roger Strauss III: pages 38, 90 (left), 133, 143, 146, 154, 161 (top)
    White Flower Farm/Photos by Michael Dodge: pages 105, 113, 131, 155

Watercolor garden designs © 1998 by Emma Sweeney

For Mimi

Burpee Basics: Growing Guides for Easy, Colorful Gardens
Down-to-earth handbooks for beginning gardeners

Available from Macmillan Publishing

Burpee Basics: Annuals, by Emma Sweeney
Burpee Basics: Perennials, by Emma Sweeney
Burpee Basics: Roses, by Mary C. Weaver
Burpee Basics: Bulbs, by Douglas Green

To order a Burpee catalogue:

order toll-free 1-800-888-1447
email www.burpee.com

or write:

Atlee Burpee & Co.
300 Park Avenue
Warminster, PA 18974

Contents

Foreword

Gardeners have been looking to Burpee for basic information about how to garden, as well as for the seeds and plants to implement their dreams, for almost 125 years. In one or the other of the six different catalogs we publish each year, a gardener can find just about any kind of plant his or her heart desires. Our big annual seed catalog, the *Burpee Annual,* has become a gardening Bible. (If you've never had the pleasure of paging through one, there's information in the front of this book about how to get your own free copy.)

What you hold in your hands—one of our new series of concise gardening guidebooks—is a continuation of that proud tradition of giving gardeners the essentials that they need. These handy little books have a great deal in common with seeds: Each one contains all you need to start a wonderful gardening experience, one that will grow year by year. Successful gardens are built on a constant reworking of the fundamentals. Even the most experienced gardeners, season after season, attend to the basic practices that you'll find so skillfully explained in these guides.

If you're a novice gardener, *Burpee Basics* will help you quickly find the information you need to get started; those of you who are more seasoned can use the books as invaluable reference tools to remind yourself of when to start the marigold seeds or divide the anemones, how to cut back the roses or determine the right amount of fertilizer for daffodils . . . all the details you need to keep your plants at their best.

We've made these books conveniently sized as well as easy on the eyes, hoping they'll find a valued spot not on your coffee table but on the shelf above your potting bench or in your garden workroom, right next to your seed packets, where they'll become as well-worn and comfortable in your hand as a favorite trowel or trusty clippers.

George Ball Jr.

Acknowledgments

This book, like most books, was really created by a team of people. I feel very blessed that the team behind this book is especially creative and talented.

My deepest thanks to: Laurie Barnett for the opportunity to write the book; Richard Parks, my agent and friend, who is always supportive, smart, and kind; and Barbara Berger, my editor at Macmillan, who carefully edited the text and photographs, oversaw the project, guided and cared for it and me, and had wise suggestions throughout. I'm grateful to have a talented editor and consider myself very lucky to have one who is also a brilliant artist. Thanks to Roger Straus III, photographer, for the beautiful photographs he contributed, his generosity and friendship, and his abundant good advice and to Gregory Piotrowski, for his astute technical editing. My thanks also to Susan Clarey, publisher.

I'm also grateful to Doris Straus, Mac McDermott, Julia Sweeney, Emily Lewis, Mary Phipps, Eric Swanson, Marilyn McLean, Ann Torrago, Kati Killam, and Bill Sweeney for help along the way.

And thanks to the team at Macmillan, including Sharon Lee, Nick Anderson, Laura Robbins, and Candace Levy.

Introduction

All of us who share the urge to garden imagine our beds and borders filled with color. We crave the arrival of bright green shoots of new growth in early spring, indicating that flowers are not far behind. We become ecstatic at the sight of new flower buds, waiting anxiously like new parents to see the flowers emerge and then taking photographs from all angles to record our good fortune. We are dreamy when we think of all the gardens we want to plant. The promise of beauty in the garden—and its fulfillment—keeps us happy. The plants that carry us through the range of our emotions are the perennials, the ever-faithful and always forgiving plants that are the backbone of any flower garden.

If you're new to gardening and interested in using perennials, this book will provide you with the basic information you need to plant and grow perennials. You'll get the fundamental, practical, and sound knowledge you need to start your gardening education.

To get your first garden up and growing, *Burpee Basics: Perennials* encourages you to keep in mind three things.

1. Start small, think big.

Even a small garden is the start of an ecosystem. A balanced and healthy ecosystem is good for everyone: the plants, the wildlife, the environment. Just because your daylily border is small does not mean it is insignificant.

2. Soil is everything.

Start with good soil and you're on your way to guaranteed success. Some things can be fudged in life, but not the soil. Every plant needs the right kind of soil.

3. To grow it is to know it.

Plants are great teachers, and every plant you grow will tell you what it needs. Learn from your plants, and keep a record of what they like and don't like. Also, keep using the plants that work for you. If you like hostas, use them, divide them, create more gardens with them. If you like sedum, buy more and use more. And don't be afraid to bring a new perennial into the garden. As the garden grows, so do we.

Perennials constantly remind us that the garden next year can and will be better. The perennials themselves will grow bigger and stronger, providing us with more abundant flowers. If we can provide the plants with what they require and master a few simple techniques, such as deadheading and dividing, the beauty of our perennials will far outshine our brief disappointments (perhaps one year our peonies didn't bloom at all!). We can bring our enthusiasm and hope to the perennial garden for the garden the next year, and the year after that. Hope springs eternal in the heart of the gardener—and why not? Our perennials remind us each spring when they reappear in our gardens that our faith is well warranted.

Emma Sweeney

getting
the basics

The Essentials

- Defining Perennials
- What All Plants Need: Sun, Water, Soil
- Soil Is Everything
- Plant Hardiness Zones and Why They Matter
- Tools and Supplies for the Gardener and the Garden

Defining Perennials

Plants are classified by the length of their life cycles, and plants that live for more than two years are grouped together under the term *perennials*. The word *perennial* is derived from the Latin word *perennis*, which means "perpetual or enduring." When grown in favorable conditions, perennials may live a very long time. Annuals and biennials, perennials' shorter-lived counterparts, take a year (annuals) or two years (biennials) to complete their life cycles.

Perennials, however, are much more than this: They are the backbone of a flower garden. They provide a sense of continuity in the garden landscape when they faithfully reappear year after year, emerging as tender green shoots, growing, and flowering. Although each perennial may bloom for just a few weeks, the plant's size and shape, foliage, and texture will contribute to the beauty of the garden throughout the year.

Perennials for Life

Some perennials will live for a very long time. For example, peonies (*Paeonia lactiflora*) will practically live forever and often outlive the gardener who planted them. Feverfew (*Tanacetum parthenium*), on the other hand, is a short-lived perennial. In between these two perennials are thousands of plants that live out their happy lives in a variety of ways. A well-cared for perennial may start to decline and need to be rejuvenated, which we do by "dividing" it. The process is described in Part Three, "Digging In," and it's an easy and inexpensive way to create more stock. Dividing perennials such as hostas, irises, and daylilies reinvigorates them and provides more plants.

Other perennials may continue living through subsequent generations of the seeds they set. Feverfew is short lived, but it self-seeds freely; so although the original plant will die, you'll never be without feverfew because of all the seedlings.

When Perennials Bloom

Perennials bloom, on the average, for a few weeks in the spring, summer, and fall. Some will bloom for longer periods—coreopsis, bleeding heart, purple coneflower, feverfew, and mallow are perennials that have a long bloom

You'll soon discover there's a lot of Latin in the garden world, and all plants have Latin names. Most of us, though, have no real knowledge of Latin; and these names might look like a series of jumbled letters. However, while the names may be long and complicated-sounding, they are easier to understand and remember once you learn how the Latin binomial system works.

Plants have both a common name, which can be acquired in any number of ways, and a scientific name, usually in Latin, which is its botanically accurate name. Although the common names of plants are much easier to pronounce (who can argue that "baby's breath" isn't easier to say than *Gypsophila paniculata*?), they aren't as reliable as the Latin names. The common name of a particular plant may be different from region to region, and the same common name may apply to a number of different plants. It's best to learn the scientific name whenever possible.

The binomial system is easy to understand once you've decoded it. Here are some tips:

- Plants have two names: The first name is the genus name; it tells you the plant's genus or type (a noun). The second name is the plant's species name (an adjective describing the noun). Both names are in italics, as in *Echinacea purpurea*. This plant's common name is purple coneflower (*purpurea* is the Latin word for "purple").
- When a multiplication sign (×) is inserted between the two names, this means the plant is a hybrid—a term used to describe the offspring that results from crossing two plants of different genera, species, or cultivars. Horticulturists can breed hybrids to create new forms of a plant, which often combine the best traits of the parent plants; hybrids can also occur in nature. An example of a hybrid is *Astilbe × arendsii*.
- A capitalized name in single quotation marks tells you that the plant is a cultivar, which is a horticultural variety or race. An example of a popular perennial cultivar is *Echinacea purpurea* 'Magnus'.
- Finally, you will see some botanical names that are abbreviated, as in *E. purpurea*. The first mention of a genus name in most texts is spelled out in full, whereas subsequent mentions are usually abbreviated to the first letter. The abbreviations "sp." (singular) and "spp." (plural) are shorthand for the word *species*.

Don't be intimidated by these polysyllabic words. And don't worry about pronouncing them correctly. Latin's been a dead language for a long time; and while the American Horticultural Society provides guidelines for correct pronunciation, there is no right or wrong way.

time—and some, like peonies, will bloom for a shorter period of time. You'll learn a simple technique in Part Three, known as "deadheading," that is a great way to get plants to bloom a second time.

When It's All About Ease

As you learn about perennials, you'll discover the obvious differences in plant shapes, sizes, and colors; but you'll also learn that perennials vary greatly in terms of their care and maintenance. It's good to know that many perennials are very easy to grow, requiring little from the gardener.

A LIST OF THE VERY EASIEST OF THE EASIEST PERENNIALS

The garden plan on page 50 shows you how to plant a simple bed that incorporates many of these easiest perennials.

Adam's-needle (*Yucca filamentosa*)
Bee balm (*Monarda didyma*)
Black-eyed Susan (*Rudbeckia fulgida*)
Coreopsis (*Coreopsis verticillata*)
Daylilies(*Hemerocallis* hybrids)
Feverfew (*Tanacetum parthenium*)
Lady's-mantle (*Alchemilla mollis*)

Purple coneflower (*Echinacea purpurea*)
Shasta daisy (*Leucanthemum* × *superbum*)
Siberian iris (*Iris sibirica*)
Stonecrop (*Sedum* spp.)
Yarrow (*Achillea* spp.)

Even the fussiest perennial is surprisingly forgiving. Unlike annuals, which will almost certainly die if you forget to water them regularly, many perennials may never know you forgot about them (for a short period of time, anyway). You won't want to neglect them for long, but perennials are not as maintenance-intensive as many shorter-lived plants.

You can also be flexible with perennials when you plant them. Don't worry if you accidentally planted the shorter lady's-mantle (*Alchemilla mollis*) in the back of a border behind a taller-growing border phlox (*Phlox paniculata*). You can simply dig up the plants and replant them in the areas you want them. In fact, some of the many pleasures of gardening with perennials are finding the perfect spot for each plant and, of course, making room for all the new plants.

A Word About Hostas

If you haven't come across a hosta, you've probably never gardened! Hostas are everywhere; and their popularity has led to the creation of literally thousands of cultivars, many of which are perfectly suited to the difficult task of looking good and performing well in shade. A bed of hosta plants is one of the very easiest gardens to grow and maintain; it's worth considering as your first garden, particularly if you have a lot of shade.

Combine a selection of hostas in the shade garden for a pleasing effect.

The Garden in Winter

Although most perennials are herbaceous, or nonwoody, and will die back in the fall when their stems turn brown, some perennials will stay green throughout winter. These perennials, like yucca and lilyturf, will continue looking good in the garden all winter.

Other perennials are nice in the winter garden because of their interesting seed heads. Yarrow, beardtongue, cottage pinks, and sedum form very attractive seed heads after the flowers have gone, adding to the garden's appearance in winter.

What All Plants Need: Sun, Water, Soil

What kind of soil do you have? How much sunlight will your garden receive? Will your area provide enough rainfall in the growing season? You'll need to know the answers to these questions to plan your new perennial garden and choose the right perennials for it. Although many perennials will adapt to a wide range of conditions, most perennials prefer a good soil, full sun, and water. If your environment doesn't provide these conditions, you can still grow a wide range of perennials suited for your area. The point is to know what your environment provides so you can, if necessary, make up for what it lacks.

The Sun

All plants need sunlight, and you need to know how much light your plants will receive. Observe the sun in the morning, midday, and afternoon. You have full sun if your area gets at least six hours of direct sunlight. You have partial sun (also known as partial shade) if the area receives sun half the day (about four hours). Partial shade may also be filtered or dappled light, such as under the branches of trees. Shade means the area receives fewer than four hours of direct sunlight a day. A garden under a north-facing wall or a woodland garden where low, dense branches overhang would probably have this kind of shade.

A sun-loving perennial will become leggy if it is not grown in full sun—its stems grow long and thin as the plant searches for light. Likewise, a shade-loving perennial actually prefers shade or partial shade and can get sunscorch if grown in full sun.

Water

If the environment doesn't provide your plants with enough water, you'll have to provide it for them. How much? How often? How to? These are the primary questions gardeners ask themselves. In general, you'll need to start your perennials right by helping them send roots as deeply as they can go, from the day you plant them. Deep-rooted plants have a cushion against drought, as they draw from water deep below the soil's surface. You should also make a habit of watching the weather. Know that high winds cause plants to dry out, and water accordingly. Watch for rain: If it isn't in the forecast and the top 3 to 4 inches of the soil are dry, it's time to water.

The type of soil you have will determine to a large degree how much and how often you'll need to water. Whether your area gets little rain or buckets, your soil should be free-draining—neither too clayey nor too sandy (see below to learn more about your soil). You'll see the phrase *a well-drained soil* a lot, particularly in the "Plant Portraits" section of this book; it refers to the ability of water to travel through soil at an average rate—neither too quickly nor too slowly. You can tell how well your soil drains by digging a hole about 1 foot deep and filling it with water. If it drains under 1 hour you have quick-draining soil; if it takes a few hours your soil is well-draining; if drainage takes longer than 3 hours your soil is slow-draining. Soil amendments can improve drainage.

If watering your plants on a regular basis is difficult, consider using an irrigation system with automatic starters. Determine how much water your plants need, and be prepared to make watering them an essential part of your gardening chores.

PERENNIALS FOR WET CONDITIONS

Astilbe (*Astilbe × arendsii* hybrid)
Cardinal flower (*Lobelia cardinalis*)
Forget-me-not (*Myosotis scorpioides*)
Gooseneck loosestrife (*Lysimachia clethroides*)
Japanese primrose (*Primula japonica*)

Narrow-leaved plantain lily (*Hosta lancifolia*)
Plantain lily (*Hosta sieboldiana*)
Siberian iris (*Iris sibirica*)
Solomon's seal (*Polygonatum odoratum*)
Yellow flag iris (*Iris pseudacorus*)

Soil Is Everything

A solid understanding of your soil is fundamental to gardening. The soil's texture, composition, and fertility are key issues for the gardener, making soil preparation the most important factor in growing a healthy plant. To give your perennials the right kind of soil, you first have to understand the type of soil you have.

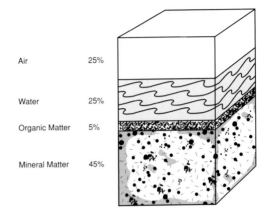

Air   25%

Water   25%

Organic Matter 5%

Mineral Matter 45%

Ratio of air, water, organic, and mineral matter in soil with good structure.

Soil has three layers: topsoil, subsoil, and bedrock. The topsoil layer is where the plants' roots get their water and nutrients. We can enrich the topsoil layer with organic matter and nutrients. The subsoil contains fewer nutrients and few soil organisms. To see the difference between topsoil and subsoil in your own garden, take a shovel or spade and dig straight down into the soil. You'll notice a marked contrast in color and in the size of the rock particles between the two layers. The subsoil is a lighter color and tends to contain bigger stones, because it is closer to the bedrock.

The goal of the gardener is to create good, healthy soil, called "loam." Loam is composed of weathered rock and mineral particles broken down over hundreds of years by water and air, and organic matter teeming with helpful microorganisms.

Sandy or Clay?

Learning about your soil's texture is a good starting point for determining how to improve it. Soil types vary, depending on the size of the soil particles. The two extreme types of soil are sand, with the largest particles, and clay, with the smallest, even microscopic, soil particles. Between the two is loam, which has a balance of both.

Find out what kind you have by digging a hole a few inches deep in slightly moistened soil and squeezing a handful of the dug-up dirt. If it has a gritty texture and falls apart easily, you have sandy soil. There are some advantages to sandy soil: Plant roots will spread easily through the light soil and drainage is good. Also, it will warm up faster in the spring. However, sandy soils drain too quickly to allow nutrients to be absorbed and are consequently not very fertile. Water rushes through a sandy soil, taking with it precious nutrients.

You've got clay soil if your soil ball is sticky and easy to mold or if it is dry, hard, and practically impossible to dig up. Clay soil won't crumble or fall apart the way sandy soil will; it contains extremely fine textured particles that hold moisture in and take the air out of the soil. Although they are often fertile with nutrients, clay soils have very poor drainage, and as a result, plant roots have a hard time establishing themselves. Water has a hard time getting through a clay soil—it drains very slowly.

Alkaline or Acid?

Another factor to take into account is the pH of a soil, which is a measure of the soil's relative "acidity" or "alkalinity." Soils that are extremely acidic or extremely alkaline prevent plants from getting the nutrients they need, because the nutrients stay locked in the soil. In other words, the plants are unable to absorb the nutrients, even if they are present in the soil. Two places where the pH tends to be extreme are deserts, which are highly alkaline, and woodland areas, where the soil can be highly acidic.

You can see from the pH scale that it runs from 14 to 0: 14.0 indicates a very high alkaline ("sweet") soil; 0 indicates a very high acid ("sour") soil. Neutral pH is 7.0, halfway between the extremes. Most perennials prefer a neutral to slightly acid pH level of 5.5 to 6.5.

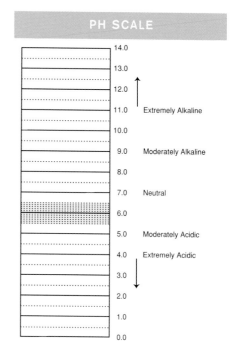

PH SCALE

14.0
13.0
12.0
11.0   Extremely Alkaline
10.0
9.0   Moderately Alkaline
8.0
7.0   Neutral
6.0
5.0   Moderately Acidic
4.0   Extremely Acidic
3.0
2.0
1.0
0.0

To test the pH of your soil, purchase a soil test kit or meter from your local hardware store or garden center. Or have your soil tested by your local Cooperative Extension, an agency within the Department of Agriculture. The soil test may be free or cost a nominal fee. A Cooperative Extension office is located in each county in the country, and you can usually find the phone number under the name of your local college. It may also be listed under the county name. If you think your soil is acid or alkaline, you should have it tested. Because conditions can change, this is a test you may want to have done every three years or so.

Building Up the Soil

Once you've determined the type of soil you have, you can work on building up its structure and fertility with organic matter. In addition to changing the structure of the soil, applications of organic matter break down over time, adding nutrients to the soil. The ultimate goal is to create fertile loam, which has dark brown color and a crumbly texture, forms a ball easily in your hand, and falls apart easily when you tap it. A loamy soil retains moisture and nutrients, and contains a balance of organic matter.

Both sandy and clay soils can be improved with organic matter. A mixture of peat moss and manure will help regulate the amount of moisture and increase the availability of nutrients in a sandy soil. Peat moss and sawdust can be added to a clay soil to lighten it up. Humus is a wonderfully useful soil amendment that will improve both sandy and clay soils. In a sandy soil, humus will help the soil retain water and nutrients; in a clay soil, humus will improve water's ability to penetrate the soil.

Soil is also improved when you add organic fertilizers (technically known as "naturally derived fertilizers"). While fertilizers and soil amendments are two different things (fertilizers feed the plants, and soil amendments improve the soil's texture and composition), some organic materials build up the soil and fertilize the plant.

NPK and TLC

There are sixteen nutrients a plant needs, and thirteen of them must come from the soil (the other three, carbon, hydrogen, and oxygen, come from the

The goal of composting is to return green matter back into organic soil; although it may take time to get the process right, it's worth trying, because the benefits are great. You'll save money in the long run on fertilizers for the garden.

The organic materials you put into the pile create what's called "humus," decomposed plant and animal matter. Humus is high in nitrogen and carbon and provides very high nutritional value for your garden.

WHAT TO USE

High Nitrogen Materials (*The Green List*)	High Carbon Materials (*The Brown List*)
Grass clippings	Leaves
Sod	Prunings from shrubs
Stems and stalks of annuals	Straw
Vegetable peelings	Ashes
Fruit pulp	Newspaper
Eggshells	Shredded bark
Coffee grounds	
Cow, horse, sheep, and chicken manures	

WHAT NOT TO USE

Meat scraps
Dairy products
Weeds and plants treated with chemicals
Pet excrement
Woody stalks

Either buy a compost bin or make one with chicken wire and stakes. Always alternate layers of brown materials and green materials, and occasionally moisten the layers with water from a hose. Turn the pile over and mix it up. The more often you turn your pile, the sooner the ingredients will have composted, leaving humus. This process should take about six months.

NATURAL FERTILIZERS AND SOIL AMENDMENTS

Fertilizers and soil amendments are not the same thing, but many organic materials fill both bills. All the items listed here are organic; the table also includes the N–P–K fertilizer value (the ratio of nitrogen, phosphorus, and

Fertilizer	Source	Fertilizer Value
Bat guano	Made from the aged manure of bats; expensive; fertilizer value varies with the source; rich in nitrogen and phosphorus; odorless	8.0–4.0–1.0
Blood meal	A by-product of the meat-packing industry; high nitrogen content; works quickly; may burn plants, so use sparingly and carefully	12.0–1.0–0
Bonemeal	A by-product of the meat-packing industry; sold as a powder; has a mild odor; high in phosphorus and low in nitrogen, thus it is most helpful for producing flowers, seeds, and roots	0.7–4.0 to 18.0–34.0 to 0
Chicken manure	Fast, strong nitrogen fix	6.0–4.0–3.0
Compost	Decomposed plant material; a gentle, slow-acting fertilizer; make your own or purchase it	1.5 to 3.5–0.5 to 1.0–1.0
Cottonseed meal	Made from the hulled seeds of cotton; ground up after the oil has been extracted	6.0–2.5–1.7
Dairy manure	Dairy cattle are pen-fed so the manure has fewer salts and fewer weed seeds than steer manure	0.25–0.15–0.25
Fish meal	Distilled from the inedible parts of commercially caught fish; thick, brown liquid; fishy smell; slow-acting source of nitrogen (released slowly to the plant roots)	10.0–4.0–0

potassium) and the soil amendment value. (**Note:** Topdressing refers to the application of an amendment to the garden soil; side-dressing should be applied specifically around the plant, as close to the roots as possible.)

Soil Amendment Value	Best Uses
None	Use as a topdressing or mix with water; good for container plants
None	Use as a side-dressing; sold as a powder—dilute and apply as a liquid; add to compost pile to speed decomposition; its unpleasant odor may deter deer
None	Good for side-dressing but expensive; steamed form is recommended over the raw form
Improves soil texture	Better for leafy vegetables than for flowering plants; use as topdressing
Improves soil's ability to hold moisture and nutrients	Apply each spring as a topdressing and work into the soil
Improves moisture retention	Highly acid; best for acid-loving plants as a topdressing; avoid applying to seedlings and small plants, as they can be burned by its direct application
Loosens soil; improves drainage in clay soil; adds texture to sandy soil	Use to improve organic content in soil. Apply in spring as a topdressing and work into the soil.
None	Dilute the concentrated form and spray on leaves for a foliar feeding

continues

Fertilizer	Source	Fertilizer Value
Humus	Rich, dark, uniformly textured substance; made from the decomposition of plant and animal matter in the final stages of decay (unlike compost, which is only partially decayed)	None
Leaf mold	Nearly decomposed compost of tree leaves	0.8–0.35–0.15
Lime	Becomes chalk in its softest form and marble at its densest and hardest; an almost pure source of calcium carbonate, which acts to de-acidify soil	None
Manures, general	Commercial types include steer, dairy, llama, and elephant manure and even zoo poop; fertilizer and soil amendment values vary with the source; llama manure is high in phosphorus and potassium, has no unpleasant odor (the llama has three stomachs so food is completely digested and converted into a great fertilizer); read labels for fertilizer content	Varies
Mushroom compost	Easy and inexpensive in areas where the mushroom-growing industry thrives	0.4 to 0.7–60.0–0.5 to 1.5
Peat	Also known as peat mulch, sphagnum peat moss, and sphagnum peat; dried and decomposed plant debris from wetlands; fibrous or powdery texture; can be difficult to wet	1.5 to 3.0–0.25 to 0.5–1.0
Seabird guano	Aged manure of seabirds; great source of phosphorus and calcium, which promotes strong roots and stems and improves disease resistance	1.0–10.0–0
Seaweed extract	Also known as kelp, kelp meal, and liquefied seaweed; rich in minerals and won't burn plants	1.0–0–1.2

Soil Amendment Value	Best Uses
Improves soil aeration and allows water to penetrate more easily in clay soil; improves sandy soil's ability to retain water	Work into soil to improve both sandy and clay soil
Improves soil's moisture and nutrient retention	Use as a mulch and dig into the soil after the growing season to improve organic content of soil
None	Use primarily to raise a soil's pH; good sources include dolomitic limestone and mushroom compost; use as a side-dressing
Loosens soil, improves drainage in a clay soil, and adds texture to a sandy soil	Incorporate into the soil in spring; some manures may deter deer
Loosens soil and improves drainage in clay soil; adds texture and volume to sandy soil	Highly alkaline; don't use around acid-loving plants; use as a side-dressing to improve soil's pH balance
Loosens clay soils and helps sandy soils retain water	Work into soil to improve it; don't use peat when it's dry; once wet, it will retain water better than any other amendment
None	Use as a topdressing
Stimulates growth of soil microbes and earthworms; expensive	Apply to the garden as topdressing each spring and fall; good source of trace minerals, plant hormones, and vitamins

continues

Fertilizer	Source	Fertilizer Value
Sewage sludge	Created from municipal sewage and aerated in a special process; looks like a rich soil mix and does not smell; popular brand name is Milorganite; some products may contain pesticides and heavy metals—read labels carefully	5.0–3.0–7.0
Steer manure	Not the best available manure; often high in salts and full of weed seeds	0.25–0.15–0.25
Wood ashes	Taken from a fireplace or wood stove; similar to limestone in alkalinity; ashes from hardwoods are more alkaline than ashes from softwoods	0 to 5.0–7.0 to 2.0–3.0
Worm castings	Worm manure; high in nutrients and microorganisms	0.5–0.5–0.3

air and water). There are three primary nutrients—nitrogen (N), phosphorus (P), and potassium (K)—which you'll hear a lot about as you learn about gardening. Keep in mind that to give your plants the tender loving care (TLC) they need, you need to continually improve your soil by adding organic matter each spring.

Each of the three primary nutrients contributes in a different way to a plant's overall health. Nitrogen develops the plant's green color in the foliage and stems; phosphorus is very important in developing the flowers, seeds, roots, and fruit. Potassium helps the plant's overall development and makes the plant's stems strong. When you go to your garden supply store you will notice that different fertilizers contain different proportions of these three elements; the ratios are labeled by weight on the bag. A label that reads "10N–10P–10K" informs you that the fertilizer contains 10 percent nitrogen, 10 percent phosphorus, and 10 percent potassium—an even ratio, indicating a "balanced" fertilizer. Other fertilizers are high in one element and low or lacking in the other two. A fertilizer with a combination of all three essential elements is called "complete."

Soil Amendment Value	Best Uses
Improves sandy soil's ability to hold moisture and nutrients; loosens heavy soils	Add to gardens as a fertilizer and soil conditioner; may deter deer
Loosens clay soil, improves moisture and nutrient retention in sand	Dilute to make a "tea" by steeping it in water, then dilute again to be sure mixture is weak; it can burn plants if not diluted properly
Can improve a sandy soil; can harm a clay soil by making it even heavier	Dig into garden in late fall with lime to raise soil's pH; don't apply more than once every 3–4 years.
None	Use as a side-dressing for plants in beds and containers

Perennials have various nutritional requirements: Some are heavy feeders, which means they require more fertilizers than the average plant. Phlox, for instance, are well-known heavy feeders. On the other end of the spectrum are perennials that need little in the way of fertilizing, such as yarrow.

Organic fertilizers are sometimes applied as a "side-dressing" or a "top-dressing." The material is either spread on top of the garden soil or around the side of the plant and then lightly scratched into the soil. Some organic fertilizers can be diluted with water and applied as foliar feed. Inorganic fertilizers, too, can be applied in different ways. You can apply them in liquid form, dry powder, or time-release pellets. You can choose which fertilizer to use based on your needs. For instance, time-release fertilizers are more expensive than the other two but are worth it if it's easier for you to make one application. Liquid fertilizers are fine—just mix with water and apply according to directions. Dry powders are applied to the soil as topdressings or side-dressings. Time-release fertilizers, such as the popular Osmocote, are coated granules that dissolve when they come in contact with water.

Plant Hardiness Zones and Why They Matter

Besides knowing whether a plant prefers sun or shade and what kind of soil you have, it's important to learn about "hardiness zones" and to determine in which zone you are gardening. Plants thrive in particular temperature ranges, and you should grow perennials that are hardy in your area.

The USDA Plant Hardiness Zone Map (see page 166) breaks down the continental United States into eleven climate zones based on lowest average temperatures—the coldest zone is 1 (subarctic) and the warmest is 11 (subtropical). Cold is a factor, along with rainfall, snowfall, and the number of hours of sunlight. Heat is also a consideration. Not all perennials are well adapted to the stress of excessive heat, as in the low-lying areas of the American Southwest.

Knowing Microclimates

Zone maps are a good starting point for determining what will grow in your area, but local "microclimates" can vary a great deal, so it's useful to know of any microclimates on your property. A microclimate is a small area where growing conditions vary from the climate in the region. A south-facing wall provides more warmth than does a north-facing wall; both create microclimates, because the conditions in their immediate areas are different from those of the general region.

Tools and Supplies for the Gardener and the Garden

Before you buy your first cranesbill or contemplate the future home of your peony bed, think about the tools you will need for your new garden. Shopping for new tools and supplies can be as overwhelming for the beginner gardener as learning Latin nomenclature, and you need to have a solid understanding of garden tools and their functions.

Basically, there are tools for garden maintenance, supplies for the soil, equipment for the gardener, and products for pest and disease control. There are also the decorative and useful items for the garden itself, such as clay, concrete, wood, and synthetic containers, planters, and urns; paving materials, such as brick and flagstone; architecturally interesting trellises, fences, and gates; and obelisks and fountains. Although you'll never need all of these items, it's good to have an idea of what you will need and a basic understanding of the necessary gardening tools and supplies.

Gardening Tools

When you garden, you want to perform the basic chores—such as weeding, digging, pruning, cutting, watering, and caring for growing plants—with relative ease. By purchasing solid, well-built, long-lasting, high-quality tools and using the right tools for the job, you'll make caring for your garden a pleasant exercise rather than hard labor.

Your high-quality shears with the ergonomically shaped handles and replaceable blades may seem expensive at first, but good shears will last a long time and save you in blisters and wrist fatigue. It's important to buy quality tools. Steel-tempered tools last longest. Try a tool out in the store, weighing it and seeing whether if feels comfortable in your hand. Choose tools that are right for your size and weight, and keep them clean. You can wipe them with a rag and oil to keep them from rusting. Blades will have to be sharpened regularly, because they will become dull.

Tools are designed to handle specific chores in the garden. For instance, the fork, spade, and shovel will allow you to prepare and plant the bed and to lift out rocks from the garden. The trowel is smaller and is ideal for planting seedlings. The hoe, or cultivator, will help you in your weeding efforts as well as in cultivating the ground; the rakes are necessary for smoothing the topsoil and cleaning up leaves and other debris. Edgers are very handy for making a neat garden edge (you can also use a square-pointed spade for the same purpose), and shears will be useful for cutting back and cleaning up plants.

Pruning Shears

Also known as pruners, hand pruners, and secateurs, pruning shears look like pliers with a spring in the pivot point and two sharp blades. Good-quality shears will have small shock absorbers, and the best ones will reduce wrist

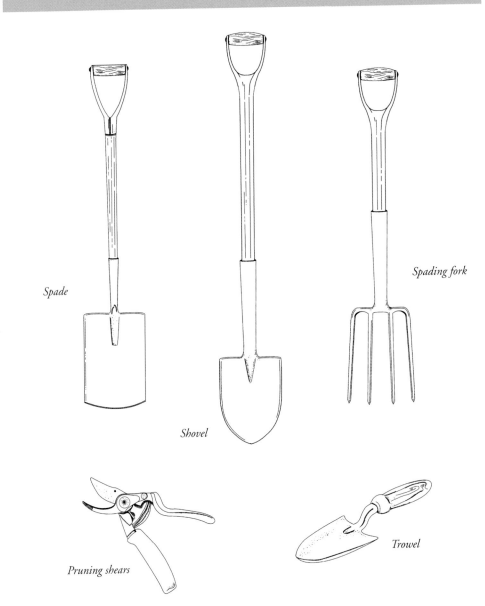

Spade

Spading fork

Shovel

Pruning shears

Trowel

fatigue. Shears are an essential tool for the gardener, and you'll use them to prune woody and green stems up to about $3/4$ inch thick.

Spading Fork

Spading forks are useful for turning over soil, lifting medium-size plants, forking in manure, and spreading mulches. You'll use this tool most often while preparing your garden bed.

Shovel and Spade

Shovels and spades come in a variety of sizes and styles, and each is designed for a particular purpose. The shovels with long handles and rounded tips are used to dig holes, scoop soil, and move plants; they have a long shank to provide better leverage. Square-pointed shovels are best used for scooping gravel. The shovel you'll need is commonly called a "garden shovel" and is somewhat smaller and lighter than these other shovels. It has a round point and is perfect for digging.

Spades come in a variety of shapes for different functions. The two most commonly used for the small garden are the square-end spade and the transplanting spade. In general, spades are like shovels in that they are also used for scooping and turning over the soil, but their smaller sizes make them more useful in the garden. The square-end spade can be used for digging, cultivating, edging, or breaking up soil.

Hoe

There are many different types of hoes. Hoes, or cultivators as they are also called, can be hand-held and attached to the end of a long shank. They are used for weeding and cultivating the soil and are available with diamond-shaped heads, flat heads, and forks with three or four tines.

Trowel

Small-scale tasks are best done with smaller tools, such as trowels. These narrow, metal scoops with curved or padded handles are ideal for transplanting seedlings. This is an item you won't want to skimp on: Get the best! Some trowels come with lifetime guarantees. You can't imagine how many trowels you may go through (in a lifetime) if you don't buy one that is built to last.

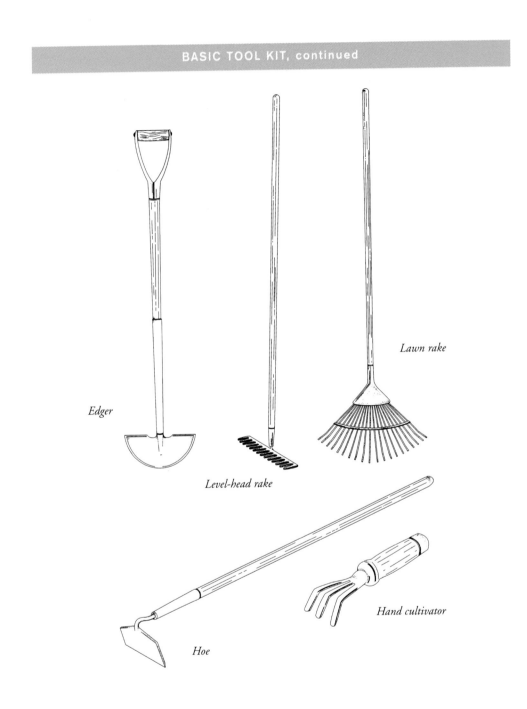

Edger

Lawn rake

Level-head rake

Hoe

Hand cultivator

Tip for Small Tools: Paint the handles of small tools with bright colors so you can easily find them in the soil.

Rake

Both lawn rakes and level-head rakes are important in the garden. The lawn rake is useful for raking leaves, twigs, grass clippings, and other light debris. Rakes made of bamboo are not as expensive as metal rakes and do the job as well. The natural feel and smell of the bamboo are nice. Be sure to store a bamboo lawn rake in a dry place.

Level-head rakes are useful for making a level surface on new garden beds and seedbeds. If you decide to get just one rake, make it the lawn rake, which you can use in the garden in a pinch.

Edger

The semicircular head on the edger is about 8 inches wide and is attached to a long handle. Edgers are ideal for cutting sharp borders along garden beds, lawn walkways, driveways, and sidewalks. Stainless steel tends to slice through sod more easily than do other metals.

Watering Tools

Get a durable, flexible, and weather-resistant rubber garden hose fitted with brass couplings that won't leak, a nozzle, and plastic watering cans.

Garden supplies you may want to think about getting later:

- Twine
- A soaker hose, which allows the water to be evenly distributed in the soil
- A dandelion weeder
- Stakes
- Labels for plants
- A barometer—it's always good to watch the weather
- A wheelbarrow

Supplies for the Garden

When you shop for your garden supplies, you'll see all kinds of amendments and conditioners for the soil as well as potting soils, mulches, and pest and disease products. Before you purchase any of these items, learn what kind of soil you have.

Containers

If your new garden will be on a city terrace, balcony, or roof garden, you will need to become acquainted with containers. Containers filled with fragrant lilies can turn a dingy black-tar rooftop into an urban oasis. Containers are also useful in the garden: Place a container filled with flowers in a bare spot in your perennial bed. The right containers are essential ornaments for any garden—big or small, urban or rural.

Materials for containers vary widely. Clay, plastic, fiberglass, concrete, wood, and cast stone are just a few choices. Some dry out faster than others and require more frequent waterings (concrete and terra-cotta, for instance, are more porous than their synthetic counterparts; they are also liable to crack from freezing and thawing and need to be brought inside in the winter). You may also want to consider some of the newer materials on the market that look remarkably like the real thing: Therma-Lite, for instance, looks just like heavy concrete or clay but is a synthetic. It not only retains moisture but is also relatively light and is thus easy to move around.

Perennials are fine in containers, as long as the container is deep enough and large enough—the plant and its roots need room to grow to mature size. Perennials with deep taproots will benefit from deep pots; whiskey barrels are

---

SHOPPING CHECKLIST

- Get solid, steel-tempered or stainless-steel tools: Spading fork, spade, shovel, trowel, hoe, steel rake, tined rake, pruning shears, and edger
- Get the right clothes—hat, light clothing, and sunblock
- Think about soil amendments, fertilizers, and mulches
- Think about containers, trellises, and benches

ideal for more shallow-rooted plants, such as lilies. Keep in mind that a larger container will provide the plant with the warmth of its insulation all winter and will allow it to stay cool in the summer.

Equipment for the Gardener

Protective clothing and gear are important in the garden. Here's a list of what you'll need and what you may want:

- A wide-brimmed hat
- An apron with pockets for hand tools
- Gardening clogs or boots
- A blank book to record notes about the garden
- A basket or bucket to carry tools in
- Sunscreen
- Garden gloves—cowhide for cooler months and bigger jobs and cotton or rubber for light tasks in the summer months

planning the garden

The Essentials

Start Small, Think Big

"Admire large gardens, start a small garden" is a gardening maxim the beginner gardener shouldn't ignore. A small bed or border—50 or 60 square feet—is just the right size for first-time perennial gardeners. In the future, you can expand on existing gardens and create more ambitious borders (traditional English perennial borders were often 100 feet long! A staff of gardeners helped . . .) as your time and enthusiasm allows. Let your confidence in gardening grow with your plants.

As you think about your new garden and begin to get an idea of what you want, look around you for inspiration. You will find it in your neighbors' gardens; in parks, public gardens, and arboretums; and in magazines and books. Mail-order catalogs from nurseries that offer seeds and young perennial plants are also a great source for learning about plants. Many catalogs offer suggestions for plant combinations and often include color illustrations of the plants in their garden settings so you can begin to get a feeling for the color combinations you like and the sizes and shapes of plants that appeal to you. Jot down your preferences in a gardening notebook and start to imagine what you want your garden to look like and where you'll put it.

When Perennials Bloom

Consider when you want your garden to be at its most glorious. Perennials bloom at different times throughout the spring, summer, and fall, usually for three to four weeks. Some perennials naturally bloom for long periods, like purple coneflower (*Echinacea purpurea*), or short periods, like peonies (*Paeonia lactiflora*). You may long for color after a drab winter and want a spring garden. Plan this garden along a path or near a doorway so you can enjoy it on your way in and out of the house. For long continuous bloom, try a border filled with daylilies and daffodils—an extra-easy and pretty combination—that starts flowering in spring with the daffodils and is carried through the early summer with the bright colors of the daylily flowers. You can choose a variety of daylilies to extend the flowering time all the way through the summer. This is the perfect garden to site along a driveway.

If you're drawn to the idea of an easy perennial garden, plan a garden filled with the *easiest* perennials, those that don't require as much time and main-

SPRING-FLOWERING PERENNIALS

Basket-of-gold (*Aurinia saxatalis*)
Bearded iris (*Iris* hybrids)
Bleeding-heart (*Dicentra eximia*)
Blue false indigo (*Baptisia australis*)
Bluestar (*Amsonia tabernaemontana*)
Catmint (*Nepeta* × *faassenii*)
Columbine (*Aquilegia* hybrids)
Cranesbill (*Geranium* spp.)

Forget-me-not (*Myosotis scorpioides*)
Goatsbeard (*Aruncus dioicus*)
Heuchera (*Heuchera* spp.)
Lady's-mantle (*Alchemilla mollis*)
Peony (*Paeonia lactiflora*)
Siberian bugloss (*Brunnera macrophylla*)
Solomon's seal (*Polygonatum odoratum*)

SUMMER-FLOWERING PERENNIALS

Astilbe (*Astilbe* × *arendsii*)
Balloon flower (*Platycodon grandiflorus*)
Beardtongue (*Penstemon digitalis*)
Bellflower (*Campanula persicifolia*)
Black-eyed Susan (*Rudbeckia fulgida*)
Border phlox (*Phlox paniculata*)
Cardinal flower (*Lobelia cardinalis*)
Daylily (*Hemerocallis* hybrids)
Feverfew (*Tanecetum parthenium*)
Globe thistle (*Echinops ritro*)

Meadow sage (*Salvia* × *superba*)
Obedient plant (*Physostegia virginiana*)
Ozark sundrop (*Oenothera missouriensis*)
Purple coneflower (*Echinacea purpurea*)
Russian sage (*Perovskia atriplicifolia*)
Speedwell (*Veronica* spp.)
Stoke's aster (*Stokesia laevis*)
Threadleaf coreopsis (*Coreopsis verticillata*)
Yarrow (*Achillea* spp.)

FALL-FLOWERING PERENNIALS

Boltonia (*Boltonia asteroides*)
Bugbane (*Cimicifuga racemosa*)
False sunflower (*Heliopsis helianthoides*)
Frikart's aster (*Aster* × *frikartii*)
Goldenrod (*Solidago* hybrids)
Japanese anemone (*Anemone* × *hybrida*)

Lilyturf (*Liriope muscari*)
Plumbago (*Ceratostigma plumbaginoides*)
Shasta daisy (*Leucanthemum* × *superbum*)
Sneezeweed (*Helenium autumnale*)
Stonecrop (*Sedum* spp.)

tenance as other plants, so you can relax in a hammock. At the end of this section you'll find seven garden plans—all under 60 square feet. One of them uses the easiest perennials.

Siting the Garden

When siting your garden, keep in mind that you ought to have a water source within 50 feet. Beyond this basic premise, you may choose the sunniest spot for your sun-loving perennials or a shady nook you want to brighten up with some white-flowering plants. Situate your garden to incorporate favorite elements, such as a massive oak or existing hydrangea shrub, a stream or a pond, or even an attractive rocky outcrop.

If you're reviving an existing perennial bed or working in a small space, think about making some modifications to the area. For instance, to allow for more sunlight, you may need to trim overhanging branches that have grown dense.

WHERE TO USE PERENNIALS

- In borders against a wall, hedge, or fence
- In specialized gardens, such as woodland, rock, Xeriscape™, meadow, or water
- To brighten a shady nook
- As a hedge
- In the cutting garden for fresh flowers
- In containers

Finally, gardeners with specific concerns may need to make these their first priority. If you have children, you don't want peonies and irises where you plan to put a baseball diamond. Try to find some borders around the house or garage for your gardens. Elderly gardeners and those with physical limitations may want their gardens easily accessible. If you entertain frequently or often have weekend guests, a cutting garden may be just the thing to provide an endless supply of fresh flowers for the house.

Here are just a few of the great perennials for cutting gardens:

Astilbe (*Astilbe* × *arendsii*)

Baby's breath (*Gypsophila paniculata*)

Black-eyed Susan (*Rudbeckia fulgida*)

Boltonia (*Boltonia asteroides*)

Cardinal flower (*Lobelia cardinalis*)

False sunflower (*Heliopsis helianthoides*)

Foxglove (*Digitalis purpurea*)

Garden mum (*Dendranthema* × *grandiflorum*)

Iris (*Iris* hybrids)

Lady's-mantle (*Alchemilla mollis*)

Peony (*Paeonia lactiflora*)

Purple coneflower (*Echinacea purpurea*)

Yarrow (*Achillea* spp.)

Tips for the best cut flowers:

- Cut flowers early in the morning when it is still cool.
- Bring a bucket of water and shears with you, cut a long stem, and place the stem in the bucket.
- Before you arrange the plants in a vase, neatly trim the leaves off the bottom ends of the stems.
- To prolong flower life, change the water daily and mist the flowers. After a day or so, cut the stem again.

Each Garden Is a Room

Finally, think of each perennial garden you create as a "room." Whether your new garden is on a city terrace or in a large backyard, plan it with the idea of creating a finished look to that part of the landscape. Garden rooms may lead into other garden rooms (as you create them in future years). Entice your guests with a rustic gate or winding path that guides them into the next garden. Even if your gardening space is limited, you may want to keep the idea of garden rooms in mind. A garden along the driveway can later be adjoined to a garden bed in front of the house.

Garden Styles

Consider your landscape as a whole: Where will your garden fit into the big picture? Is the house modern or traditional? Big or small? Your garden should complement your home and its architecture.

Think about the shape of the bed itself. Do you want to design a border (a garden backed by a wall, fence, or shrubs) for your perennials? Or do you want an island bed (a garden that is viewed from all angles, perhaps placed in the middle of the lawn)? These are a few of the decisions you'll begin to work out as you design your perennial garden.

Perennials in a Formal Setting

A formal garden has an overall look of neatness and tidiness about it. The principles underlying its design are symmetry, order, angles, pattern, and repetition: A rectangular hedge of neatly clipped boxwoods encloses peonies, lavender, dianthus, and irises. These plants, like the boxwoods, are perfect for the formal garden because their shapes are compact or, in the case of the iris with its stiff, swordlike foliage, make strong visual impact. Plants in the formal garden, like hostas and sedum, are generally tidy plants that do not sprawl or become invasive.

Formal houses—like formal gardens—are defined by their use of symmetry and angles. These houses usually have a kind of "boxy" architecture. Homes with formal touches, like those with cylindrical or square pillars in the front, dictate the need for similar treatment in the landscape.

Informal or Casual Gardens

An informal garden is filled with perennials that seem to spill out of the garden and sprawl over everything in sight. You won't find a formal hedge around this garden. Plants in the informal garden tend to have a relaxed habit about them, like plants with daisy-shaped flowers, such as black-eyed Susans, purple coneflowers, and Shasta daisies. Or plants with an airy, cottage-like feeling, such as hollyhocks and mallow. The informal border may be backed by a rustic split-rail fence, and the front edge is often free-form, shaped to imitate the natural contours of the terrain. Informal houses, such as a rambling colonial or a California bungalow, are likely to require a more informal garden. The appeal of these houses is in their meandering layouts and open floor plans.

Letting Nature In

Beyond these considerations of formal or informal, bed or border, think about using plants in your design that are native in your area. By choosing plants endemic to your region—such as sedums in dry, western gardens; asters in northeast gardens; and purple coneflower in the prairie states—you'll create a garden that's easy to maintain, because the plants' cultural needs match the growing conditions in your garden. False sunflower, golden-rod, gayfeather, and butterfly weed are midwestern natives, and sweeps of these flowers in a prairie-like setting are perfect in a midwestern garden.

Sometimes we have no choice but to let nature guide us in the decisions we make about the plants we grow. We can try to bend nature to our will, but in the end we'll be fighting an uphill battle, manifest when the sun-loving peonies growing under the shade of tall trees become leggy in their search for sunlight. There are plenty of ways to work with nature and to accommodate a particularly dry or shady region or even a very small space. Here are some solutions.

The Dry Garden

Gardeners in the desert and semiarid regions of the United States have to make the best of low rainfall and prolonged drought conditions. Here are some ways to get the most from a dry garden:

- Make use of plant species that require little, if any, water beyond what naturally occurs as rain or snow. Good garden design can reduce waterings.
- Avoid planting on top of a slope, as water naturally runs off.
- Make use of shaded areas, such as the north sides of buildings; and try not to plant in windy areas.
- Give your garden a soil that can retain water, one that is neither too sandy nor too clayey.

- Put thirsty plants in one area of the garden, plants that require less water in another. Take into account microclimates, making the best of naturally cool spots, such as north-facing walls and shady areas.
- Use a mulch to keep your soil cool and moist in the summer.
- Water only when absolutely necessary.

These perennials stand up well in the heat of zones 9 and 10.

Black-eyed Susan (*Rudbeckia fulgida*)

Blanketflower (*Gaillardia* × *grandiflora*)

Cranesbill (*Geranium* spp.)

Daylily (*Hemerocallis* hybrids)

False sunflower (*Heliopsis helianthoides*)

Plumbago (*Ceratostigma plumbaginoides*)

Threadleaf coreopsis (*Coreopsis verticillata*)

Yarrow (*Achillea* spp.)

Too Much Shade

If you think your new garden may be too shady, try to add some light or reflected light in the following ways:

- Thin trees
- Paint walls white
- Add white pebbles to a path

Too Much Sun

Even the greatest sun-lover needs a respite now and then from the sun, and you may want to add a shady spot to your yard. Here are some ways to enjoy a bit of shade:

- Add trellises and arbors, and plant vines and roses to clamber up and cover them.
- Plant hedges or tall trees on the south side of the garden.

These perennials tolerate partial or full shade, such as that of overhanging trees or buildings:

Astilbe (*Astilbe* × *arendsii*)

Bleeding-heart (*Dicentra eximia*)

Forget-me-not (*Myosotis scorpioides*)

Goatsbeard (*Aruncus dioicus*)

Heuchera (*Heuchera* spp.)

Hosta (*Hosta* spp.)

Japanese anemone (*Anemone* × *hybrida*)

Japanese iris (*Iris ensata*)

Japanese primrose (*Primula japonica*)

Lily-of-the-valley (*Convallaria majalis*)

Lilyturf (*Liriope muscari*)

Siberian bugloss (*Brunnera macrophylla*)

Solomon's seal (*Polygonatum odoratum*)

Sweet violet (*Viola odorata*)

When Every Inch Counts

If your new garden is in a small space, such as a small backyard or terrace, consider the following:

- Keep color to a minimum.
- Use perennials with nice foliage, such as hostas and astilbes, that look good when not flowering.
- Install a trellis along the wall and grow vines to add the dimension of height to the area.

Container Gardens

Containers are great places for many perennials, especially for rooftop and terrace gardens or where the soil is unworkable:

- Use large containers—your perennials are going to live and grow in them for long time.
- Give the plants a suitable location in sun or shade, with the proper soil, and plenty of water. Remember, your perennials growing in containers

rely on you for all their needs. (See "Planting Perennials in Containers," page 73, for information about what potting medium to use.)

- Elevate larger containers to expose drainage holes; bricks work well.
- Move containers around if they are getting too much or too little sun or if the soil dries out too fast.
- Use colorful pots with discretion—let the plants make the statement.

The Mixed Border: A Harmonious Blend of Perennials, Shrubs, and Annuals

Mixed borders are those that combine perennials, annuals, and shrubs in the same garden to good effect. Although these aren't traditional perennial borders, they are often the most practical if you want a large garden. Shrubs can add dimension and ballast to a garden and need relatively little care. They also offer color with their flowers, fruits, or leaves. For some great shrubs in the garden try butterfly bush (*Buddleia davidii*), barberry (*Berberis thunbergii* 'Atropurpurea Nana'), and cinquefoil (*Potentilla fruticosa*).

Annuals are a great addition to the newly planted perennial bed. It may be a few years before your perennials grow to full size, and in the first year, annuals can help fill in the bare spots. You can also plant annuals throughout the year wherever you find empty spaces in the garden: They can be used to replace a perennial that has died or to camouflage raggedy foliage on a perennial. Add annuals such as these to your perennial bed: ageratum (*Ageratum houstonianum*), heliotrope (*Heliotropium arborescens*), stock (*Matthiola incana*), lobelia (*Lobelia erinus*), French marigold (*Tagetes patula*), and nasturtium (*Tropaeolum majus*).

Working with Color

One of the most famous gardens known for its color is the impressionist painter Claude Monet's Giverny outside of Paris. The artist chose his flowers for their colors and was not afraid to break with convention, often by combining colors, flowers, and shapes that were unusual but always pleasing. We can take a lesson from Monet's garden if we will let our artist's eye guide us in creating our own gardens.

Some Color Concepts

No doubt Monet's artistic sensibility and vast experience with color put him at a great advantage. Understanding a few basic ideas about how to use color will help give you some insight into designing your garden.

Hot and bright colors—such as the reds, oranges, and yellows in beebalm, Ozark sundrops, and black-eyed Susans—tend to look their best in large spaces that they can't overwhelm. Colors on this side of the spectrum are said to "advance." That is, they appear larger and closer than they really are.

On the other side of the color spectrum are the cold or cool colors: blues, purples, and greens. These colors are said to "recede"; they look smaller and farther away than they really are. Cool colors give the illusion of space, making a small garden appear bigger.

You can use these effects in your own garden to make it appear larger or smaller, or closer or farther away, than it actually is. The colors you choose

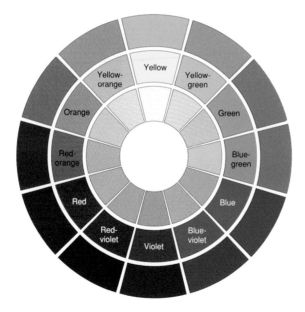

The color wheel shows primary colors (red, yellow, blue) and the colors that connect them (red-yellow, or orange, for instance). Hues are pure colors; shades are made by the addition of black, and tints, by the addition of white.

can also help set the kind of mood you want: Blues, greens, lavenders, and grays establish a serene and tranquil setting; whereas the hotter colors are lively and energetic.

Combining Colors

Consider the effects of colors used singly and combined with other colors. For instance, when we use just one color in a garden (called a monochromatic color scheme), we can introduce a feeling of restraint and formality. A garden with white roses is simple, elegant, formal. In a polychromatic color scheme, several colors are used to create a vibrant, kinetic picture. Placing colors of different values—blues next to yellows next to violets, for instance—can be a challenge for the garden designer, but the results can be wonderful. A riot of color is exciting.

When we use two colors that sit next to each other on the color wheel, we are using colors that are said to harmonize. The combination of these colors—blue and green, for instance—creates a restful picture: Your eye is allowed to view the entire scene without stopping to refocus. When we use colors that sit directly across from each other on the color wheel, so-called complementary colors, the opposite effect is obtained: The picture is more

Border designed with harmonious colors.   *Border designed with complementary colors.*

BLUE FLOWERS

Balloon flower (*Platycodon grandiflorus*)
Bellflower (*Campanula* spp.)
Blue African lily (*Agapanthus africanus*)
Bluestar (*Amsonia tabernaemontana*)
Cranesbill (*Geranium* 'Johnson's Blue')
Forget-me-not (*Myosotis scorpioides*)
Frikart's aster (*Aster × frikartii*)
Globe thistle (*Echinops ritro*)

Iris (*Iris* hybrids)
Meadow sage (*Salvia × superba*)
Monkshood (*Aconitum carmichaelii*)
Pincushion flower (*Scabiosa caucasica*)
Plumbago (*Ceratostigma plumbaginoides*)
Russian sage (*Perovskia atriplicifolia*)
Speedwell (*Veronica* spp.)

YELLOW FLOWERS

Basket-of-gold (*Aurinia saxatalis*)
Black-eyed Susan (*Rudbeckia fulgida*)
Blanketflower (*Gaillardia × grandiflora*)
Butterfly weed (*Asclepias tuberosa*)
Daylily (*Hemerocallis* hybrids)
False sunflower (*Heliopsis helianthoides*)
Goldenrod (*Solidago* hybrids)

Iris (*Iris* hybrids)
Lady's-mantle (*Alchemilla mollis*)
Mullein (*Verbascum × hybridum*)
Ozark sundrops (*Oenothera missouriensis*)
Threadleaf coreopsis (*Coreopsis verticillata*)
Yarrow (*Achillea* spp.)

PINK FLOWERS

Astilbe (*Astilbe × arendsii*)
Balloon flower (*Platycodon grandiflorus*)
Bee balm (*Monarda didyma*)
Bleeding-heart (*Dicentra spectabilis*)
Boltonia (*Boltonia asteroides*)
Border phlox (*Phlox paniculata*)
Columbine (*Aquilegia* hybrids)
Cottage pink (*Dianthus plumarius*)
Foxglove (*Digitalis* spp.)

Heuchera (*Heuchera* spp.)
Hollyhock mallow (*Malva alcea*)
Japanese anemone (*Anemone × hybrida*)
Obedient plant (*Physostegia virginiana*)
Peony (*Paeonia lactiflora*)
Prairie mallow (*Sidalcea malviflora*)
Stoke's aster (*Stokesia laevis*)
Stonecrop (*Sedum* spp.)

dazzling. Complementary color schemes—yellow and blue, for instance, or purple and orange—allow both colors to be used to their best advantage.

Last, it is helpful to think about backdrops when considering how to contrast color in your garden. A green hedge, for instance, will bring out the colors in a perennial border, particularly the lighter and paler colors. Remember, too, that there are many different shades of green. A row of emerald green evergreens is dramatic, as it highlights and complements colors in the border it backs; shrubs with gray-green foliage provide a less intense contrast to the colors in the garden.

White in the Garden

White is an important color in the garden: We all know how useful white sprays of baby's breath are to a florist. White or cream flowers can tone down hot colors, such as red, and are often helpful as a buffer between two plants. If you're not sure whether your pink phlox (*Phlox paniculata*) will look good next to your red bee balm (*Monarda didyma*), plant white-flowering Shasta daisies (*Leucanthemum* × *superbum*) between the two plants.

A word of caution on using white in the garden: Use it in small doses and repeat plantings throughout the garden. One big splash of white in a border of colorful flowers often looks like a hole where color should be and isn't. But if you scatter white throughout, it will create a feeling of unity in the landscape. Other wonderful white-flowering perennials are boltonia, baby's breath, bugbane, white-flowering astilbes, and spires of white-flowering foxglove.

Color and Light

Remember that color is only as good as the light it appears in. Think about the way the color red looks in bright sunlight and then in shade. In sunlight, red is bright as fire, vibrant, exciting, energized. In shade, red can be so nearly black as to disappear. You'll notice, too, that on a more subtle level sunlight is different, depending on where you are in the world. As we near the equator, the sun's light grows more intense—brighter and stronger. As we move away from the equator, toward cooler regions, light grows softer, more diffuse. It's worth noting that colors brighten or soften, depending on where they are and how much sunlight is on them.

The Shape of Things

The heights and shapes of perennials are factors in creating your garden. Think about placing your plants in the garden according to their sizes, but don't be dogmatic about this. In general, taller plants are best in the back of a border or toward the center of an island bed, and smaller, low-growing plants work best as edgings. But a garden simply arranged from shortest to tallest can look uninspired. Try a taller plant toward the front, just to break up the order. Weave a plant throughout the garden to create a flowing feeling. Most important, design your garden using groups of plants in uneven numbers—threes, fives, sevens—because the asymmetry causes them to cohere in a pleasingly aesthetic way. Plants grouped in even numbers tend to look like they were paired in twos, and such groups look more static to the eye. Finally, use one "accent" plant with interesting foliage (yuccas make great accent plants) to draw the eye to a specific area of the garden.

Consider a plant's shape. Is it billowy like baby's breath, with a loose, informal feeling? Or is it more rigid and imposing, like an iris with stiff, swordlike foliage? Think about how your plants will measure up when placed beside each other, and keep in mind shapes and sizes when designing your perennial bed.

AESTHETICS IN THE GARDEN

Don't forget to add architectural interest (and a bit of whimsy) to your garden. Consider birdbaths, purple martin houses, bird feeders, gargoyles, Victorian gazing balls, sundials, weathered urns, wooden obelisks, and concrete urns.

Flower Shapes

Flower shapes and clusters, or "inflorescences" as they are called, come in many forms and sizes, including composite (daisy), raceme, spike, umbel, and panicle. Using plants with different flower shapes and complementary colors can be striking: Plant the blue daisy flowers of Frikart's aster (*Aster* ×

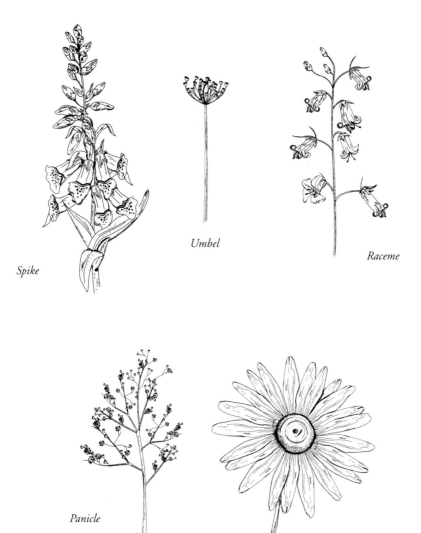

Spike

Umbel

Raceme

Panicle

Composite

frikartii) beside stonecrop (*Sedum* 'Autumn Joy') with its dense clusters of pink-tinged flowers. Plant yarrow (*Achillea* 'Moonshine') with its yellow corymbs next to the spiky blue flowers of meadow sage (*Salvia* × *superba*). In both cases, the shape and color of the plant are enhanced by those of the plant beside it.

Foliage Matters

A plant's foliage—its color, shape, and texture—is a significant design element; this is particularly true with perennials, since flowers are only part of their attraction. Consider how different the big, bold, bluish green leaves of some of the hosta plants are compared to the filigreed, gray-green leaves of wormwood (*Artemisia ludoviciana*) or the fernlike foliage of threadleaf coreopsis (*Coreopsis verticillata*). Use a mix of foliage textures and colors in the garden. Combine catmint (*Nepeta* × *mussinii*) with its finely cut, aromatic foliage, with lamb's ears (*Stachys byzantina*), which has big soft and fuzzy leaves.

The bold leaves of these hosta plants are perfectly suited for this shady walkway.

Adam's-needle (*Yucca filamentosa*)

Astilbe (*Astilbe × arendsii*)

Blue false indigo (*Baptisia australis*)

Bleeding-heart (*Dicentra spectabilis*)

Bugbane (*Cimicifuga racemosa*)

Colewort (*Crambe cordifolia*)

Cranesbill (*Geranium* spp.)

Daylily (*Hemerocallis* hybrids)

Heuchera (*Heuchera* spp.)

Hosta (*Hosta* spp.)

Iris (*Iris* hybrids)

Japanese anemone (*Anemone × hybrida*)

Lady's-mantle (*Alchemilla mollis*)

Lamb's ears (*Stachys byzantina*)

Lilyturf (*Liriope muscari*)

Mullein (*Verbascum* hybrids)

Peony (*Paeonia lactifolia*)

Siberian bugloss (*Brunnera macrophylla*)

Planning and Mapping the Garden

The first step in planning and mapping your perennial garden is to lay it out in your yard. You can do this with measuring tape and string to indicate straight lines and a garden hose or rope flexed in the desired shape to mark curved beds or borders. You will be drawing two maps: The first is a sketch of the site, which you will make outdoors, and the second is a garden plan, which you can draw later using the information you have gathered outside.

Planning

You've already chosen the site for your garden. The next step is to sketch an overhead view, in a notebook, on site. Use the measuring tape to measure the length and width of the potential bed, but certainly don't get bogged down in the detail of measuring the longer distances; wherever you can, pace off distances. You should feel free to be as basic as you can: Just draw straight lines to indicate where the borders of the garden are. Draw curved lines if the bed has a curved shape.

Assess how much sun your new garden will have by determining the polar directions. Where is your garden when you face north? Note on your sketch pad the direction north (it's easiest if you designate this on the paper with an arrow facing up, making north up, south down, east to the right, and west to the left). Include other relevant features in your sketch, such as a rough outline of your house (indicate where windows and doors are) trees, shrubs, existing gardens, paths, and fences.

Finally, note how much sun your garden will get: full sun, shade, or partial shade. Record all the information you gather on your sketch pad. This survey will provide you with a record for years and will help you design and plan new gardens.

Your survey could turn up some surprises. Perhaps you thought your garden was in full sun and learn that, in fact, a portion of the garden is in partial shade. You may have forgotten an existing large shrub and now have to decide whether to incorporate it into the design, resite the garden, or get rid of the shrub. Preparing a map is a great exercise for helping you learn about your site. It will also help you determine the number of plants you will need for the garden.

TAKE A PICTURE

You may also want to take photographs of your garden site at this time. If you left something out, the picture will remind you. Before and after photographs are also great incentive builders and will no doubt encourage you to create more gardens.

Mapping the Garden

The next step is to draw up a garden plan. Prepare a list of the plants that you want to use in your garden design; read through Part Four of this book to help you decide which plants to grow.

The best paper to use for your garden design is graph paper, and the best graph paper to use is made from vellum. It's easy to erase pencil marks from vellum paper (you don't get ghost lines), and it holds up well under repeated use. First, make a legend in the lower right corner of your paper, indicating the scale you are using, such as 1 inch = 1 foot. Next, draw an arrow facing up and write *north*. It's important to get your bearings, and establishing the direction of the sun is key. Finally, outline the garden you have planned. If you are designing a border that is 5 feet long and 10 feet wide, draw the outline in inches and mark the distances in feet on the grid. You may want to use a ruler to help you with the straight lines. Draw island beds and curved lines free hand. Now it's time to start planning the garden.

Each perennial will have specific spacing needs; you'll find a list of spacing requirements in the Appendix. The larger perennials, such as goatsbeard (*Aruncus dioicus*) and some hostas, need a lot of space, as much as 3 feet. Smaller perennials need 1 to 2 feet. Be as precise as you can with spacing requirements at this point to avoid making costly mistakes later on when you may get too many plants or too few.

Make a circle on your graph paper to indicate each perennial. (You can find clear plastic templates with different-size circle stencils in any art-supply store.) For instance, if 1 inch = 1 foot on your garden design and the perennial you want to use needs a 1-foot spacing, draw a circle that is 1 inch in diameter to indicate that plant. Moving through the design, make groupings of plants (ones, threes, fives) to indicate your plants in the design. Try not to create groupings of plants in rigid lines, but rather stagger the plants in each group or bend the row slightly in one direction or another. It's probably easiest to start your garden design with the largest perennials on your list, like peonies. Find a place for your peony and design the smaller plants around it. Use the design concepts discussed earlier. Repeat plants, weave plants, use plants with architectural interest to give definition to the garden. Be sure to add each plant to the legend in the lower right corner of your paper; include the plant's name, its flower color, and the number of plants you plan to use.

The plan you create on paper will provide you with a valuable blueprint for your garden. You will refer to this plan when you buy your plants (so you know just how many to get) and when planting. Hang on to the plan for the future; you may want to move perennials around and try out new combinations.

These two-dimensional plans have their limitations (there's no sense of depth or texture), but the overhead perspective of the garden gives you a good sense of the overall picture, and this stage of planning is an important step in the process toward planting the garden. You'll be surprised by how much your ability to design a garden will improve if you first work it out on paper.

Remember, refining and editing are important parts of the process, and every good plan allows for as much modification as necessary.

Seven Easy Garden Plans

If designing and planning a garden at this stage is less attractive to you than getting out there and starting to plant your garden, consider using any one of the seven garden plans that follow. You can choose from a spring border, an easy perennial border, a wildlife garden, a shady nook, a damp-soil garden, a rock garden, or an old-fashioned border.

A Spring Garden

Here's a border that comes alive in the spring; it should be planted where you can appreciate its beauty whether sitting outside or looking out from a window. The site may be along a fence near a driveway or by the front or the back door—somewhere you can have access to it without having to go far in case the weather is cold.

Choose a 5 × 10-foot area that gets full or partial sun in early spring. Remember, this garden blooms before the leaves have fully emerged on deciduous trees, so you may have more sun available than you think. A low edging of stone or bricks between the border and your lawn adds a nice ornamental touch.

PLANT LIST

A Peony (*Paeonia lactiflora*) white and pink (2)
B Blue false indigo (*Baptisia australis*) blue (3)
C Bleeding-heart (*Dicentra spectabilis*) rose (3)
D Bleeding-heart (*Dicentra spectabilis* 'Alba') white (3)
E Columbine (*Aquilegia × hybrida* 'McKana Giant') mixed (3)
F Bearded iris (*Iris* hybrids) lilac (5)
G Siberian iris (*Iris sibirica*) blue (3)
H Cranesbill (*Geranium* 'Johnson's Blue') blue (6)
I Lady's-mantle (*Alchemilla mollis*) yellow (3)
J Forget-me-not (*Myosotis scorpiodes*) blue (5)

Design for a 5 × 10-foot spring border

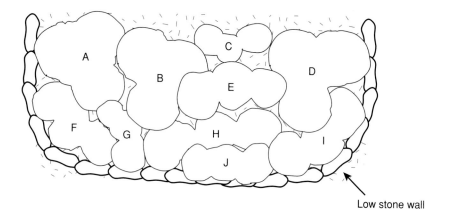

Low stone wall

The Easiest Perennial Border

Try a border that makes use of the easiest perennials. These plants are tolerant of a wide range of conditions and will provide you with great color throughout the summer. Choose a sunny site where a fence, wall, or border of evergreens or shrubs can serve as the backdrop.

PLANT LIST

A Adam's-needle (*Yucca filamentosa*) foliage (1)

B Purple coneflower (*Echinacea purpurea*) purple (3)

C Bee balm (*Monarda didyma*) red (3)

D Russian sage (*Perovskia atriplicifolia*) blue (3)

E Shasta daisy (*Leucanthemum × superbum*) white (1)

F Siberian iris (*Iris siberica*) blue (4)

G Sedum (*Sedum telephium* 'Autumn Joy') pink (3)

H Daylily (*Hemerocallis* hybrids) orange (4)

I Threadleaf coreopsis (*Coreopsis verticillata*) yellow (3)

J Catmint (*Nepeta × mussinii*) blue (3)

Design for a 5 × 10-foot easiest perennial border

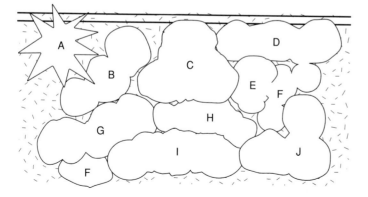

Inviting Wildlife

You can create an environment for butterflies, hummingbirds, birds, and toads by using plants and objects that attract them. Choose an area in full sun and dig a bed 6 × 11 feet. Put in birdbaths, small ponds, purple martin houses, hummingbird feeders—any kind of feature that attracts the wildlife you want. Brightly colored flowers draw hummingbirds and butterflies (especially orange and red), so if you want to use more perennials or annuals with these colors, feel free to substitute. One rule: Don't use insecticides around this garden.

PLANT LIST

A Butterfly bush (*Buddleia davidii*) blue, pink, purple (3)

B Bee balm (*Monarda didyma*) red (3)

C Purple coneflower (*Echinacea purpurea*) purple (3)

D Butterfly weed (*Asclepias tuberosa*) orange (6)

E Gay feather (*Liatris spicata*) purple (3)

F Border phlox (*Phlox paniculata*) red (3)

G Plumbago (*Ceratostigma plumbaginoides*) blue (5)

H Catmint (*Nepeta × mussinii*) lavender (5)

I Pincushion flower (*Scabiosa caucasica*) blue (4)

Design for a 6 × 11-foot wildlife garden

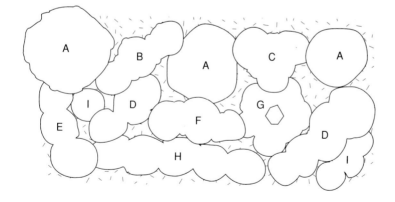

Shady Nook Garden

The shady nook garden is designed for perennials that thrive in partial or full shade. This garden is situated under a north-facing wall, but you can adapt the plan for any shady area. Choose an area in shade, and dig a 6 × 8-foot bed. Add humus and other organic matter to enrich the soil for these plants.

PLANT LIST

A Siberian bugloss (*Brunnera macrophylla*) blue (1)
B Goatsbeard (*Aruncus dioicus*) white (1)
C Plantain lily (*Hosta sieboldii*) lilac (3)
D Astilbe (*Astilbe* × *arendsii* hybrid) cream (3)
E Solomon's seal (*Polygonatum odoratum*) white (3)
F Lily-of-the-valley (*Convallaria majalis*) white (8)
G Heuchera (*Heuchera* hybrids) pink (3)

Design for a 6 × 8-foot shady nook garden

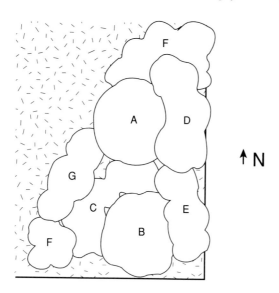

Damp-Soil Garden

Although most garden plants need a soil that drains well, there are some moisture-loving plants that thrive in a soil that remains damp. Here's an island garden that can be situated in a low spot in the lawn where water naturally collects. Dig a bed 6 × 8 feet in full sun or filtered shade. Some shade is preferable in warmer areas.

PLANT LIST

A Plantain lily (*Hosta sieboldiana*) blue foliage (2)

B Cardinal flower (*Lobelia cardinalis*) red (3)

C Astilbe (*Astilbe × arendsii*) pink (3)

D Siberian iris (*Iris sibirica*) blue (3)

E Narrow-leaf plantain lily (*Hosta lancifolia*) foliage (3)

F Japanese primrose (*Primula japonica*) mixed (3)

G Forget-me-not (*Myosotis scorpioides*) blue (11)

Design for a 5 × 10-foot damp-soil garden

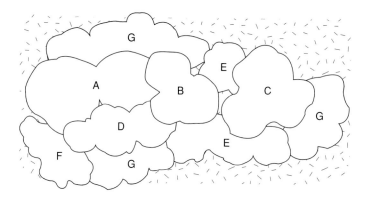

Rock Garden

You can plan a garden to take advantage of a rocky outcrop. It may be on a slope, embankment, or flat land. Use the rocks in the garden to enhance the beauty of the perennials.

Choose a sunny site where a group of rocks is visually appealing. You can rearrange some of the rocks, but most will be too heavy to lift. Just arrange the plants around the existing rocks. Add soil to the garden if there is not enough.

PLANT LIST

A Yarrow (*Achillea* 'Moonshine') yellow (2)

B Barberry (*Berberis thunbergii* 'Atropurpurea Nana') foliage (1)

C Cottage pink (*Dianthus plumarius*) white (3)

D Adam's-needle (*Yucca filamentosa*) foliage (1)

E Meadow sage (*Salvia* × *superba*) blue (1)

F Ozark sundrops (*Oenothera missouriensis*) yellow (1)

G Stonecrop (*Sedum* 'Ruby Glow') deep pink (3)

H Basket-of-gold (*Aurinia saxatalis*) yellow (3)

Design for a 5 × 11-foot rock garden

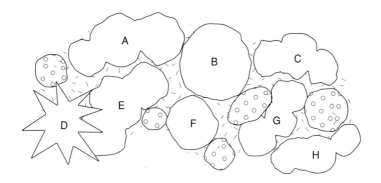

Old-Fashioned Border

Here's a garden that has the old-world charm of cottage garden plants, such as foxglove, geraniums, and lady's-mantle. Choose a site in direct sun that has a wall or fence as a backdrop and a lawn or path bordering the front. Dig a bed 10 × 4 feet. For added cottage charm, add scented roses, annuals such as sweet peas (*Lathrys odoratus*), and herbs (try rosemary and thyme).

PLANT LIST

A Oriental poppies (*Papaver orientale*) pink (3)

B Foxglove (*Digitalis × mertonensis*) mixed (3)

C Border phlox (*Phlox paniculata*) white (3)

D Russian sage (*Perovskia atriplicifolia*) lavender (1)

E Baby's breath (*Gypsophila paniculata*) white (1)

F Bellflower (*Campanula persicifolia*) white (3)

G Shasta daisy (*Leucanthemum × superbum*) white (3)

H Musk mallow (*Malva moschata*) pink (3)

I Cottage pink (*Dianthus plumarius*) white (5)

J English lavender (*Lavandula angustifolia* 'Munstead') lavender (1)

K Lamb's ears (*Stachys byzantina*) gray foliage, magenta blooms (5)

L Catmint (*Nepeta × mussinii*) lavender (3)

Design for a 5 × 12-foot old-fashioned border

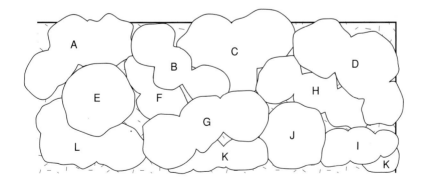

digging in

The Essentials

- Preparing the Garden Bed
- Planting Perennials
- Skills in the Garden: Watering, Feeding, Weeding
- Perennial Care: Staking, Deadheading, Dividing,
  Fall Cleanup, Winter Mulches
- The Natural Way to Healthy Plants

Preparing the Garden Bed

Lifting out rocks, weeds, old roots, and other debris from your potential garden bed is hard work—but necessary and ultimately rewarding. You learned in Part One how important it is that perennials have good, loamy soil from which to draw their nutrients. The best time to enrich the soil is when you dig and prepare the bed.

It's best to prepare the bed and improve the soil when the weather is cool, and spring and fall are the ideal times. If you can prepare the bed well in advance of planting time, you'll give the soil time to settle. Ideally, you should prepare your new bed in the fall and plant in the spring. If you haven't got time for that, prepare your new bed in the spring or fall and give it at least a month to settle before planting in it. If you plant too soon after digging up the ground, the soil will settle around the plants, leaving their roots exposed to sun and wind.

THE BED IN WINTER

If you dig and prepare your garden bed in the fall and plan to plant in the following spring, lay a mulch of compost or shredded leaves over the newly dug bed to protect the soil from exposure to strong winds and rains during the winter months. In the spring, incorporate the mulch by turning it over with your spade and digging it into the soil. Then plant your perennials.

You need the right tools to remove brush, weeds, and debris from the garden. Have on hand your spade (a straight-edged spade is best here so you can dig vertically into the soil), a fork for lifting out heavy rocks, and a rake (preferably one with a level head). You'll use the rake for the final step of grading and leveling the ground. You should also have a wheelbarrow or old sheet to haul things in and out of the garden. You'll be hauling out the debris, and carrying in the soil amendments, which, in forty-pound bags, are heavy.

Step 1: Removing the sod

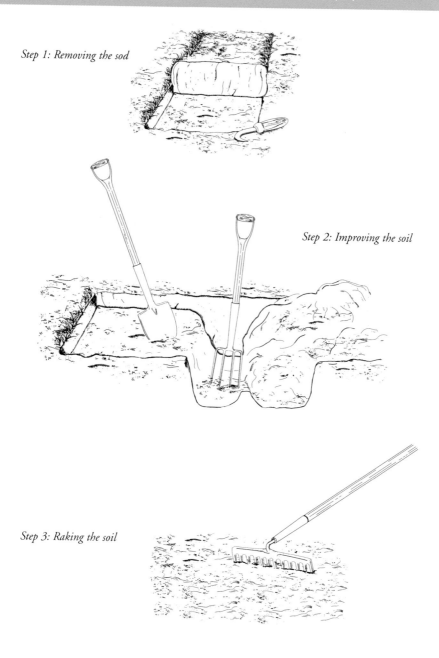

Step 2: Improving the soil

Step 3: Raking the soil

Step One: Removing the Sod

The first step in preparing the garden bed is to remove the grass and weeds. It's tempting to rush through this part of the process, but don't! You'll be plagued by pernicious weeds for years to come, and this is actually not a difficult job. Where the land has to be cleared of shrubs, large rocks, and brush, the job gets a little harder.

Rolling Up the Lawn

If you're placing your new garden in the middle of an existing lawn, you can slice up the sod and remove it, much like the way you cut a carpet and roll it up.

First, outline your garden area with stakes and string or lime. Using a sharp knife (a linoleum knife works best, which you can buy at any hard-

AVOIDING POISON IVY

If you think you might be getting into poison oak or ivy, wear gloves and a long-sleeved shirt. In areas of the country where ticks are a problem, wear light-colored pants tucked into socks.

ware store), cut into the sod as you would a carpet, pulling the knife back toward you (being very careful!). Following the outline in the sod, cut down the length of the garden bed for about 4 feet, then make a parallel cut about 2 feet away. Next, make a cut at the top that connects the ends of those two lines, forming three sides of a rectangle. Work your fingers into the connecting cut and under the sod, gently tugging at the grass. You'll feel it pry loose. If it doesn't come up right away, take your spade or edger and gently loosen it. Once you get a few inches loose, roll back the sod. You can continue this process throughout the bed, working from one end to another. Be sure to shake as much soil from the pieces of sod as you can into the garden bed. It's good topsoil and worth keeping. Pieces of sod can be put into a wheelbarrow or on an old sheet nearby and either thrown in the compost bin or placed on bare spots in the lawn where they may re-root.

Smothering with Plastic or Newspaper

If you're digging your garden when the weather will remain hot for weeks at a time (perhaps late spring or early fall), you can eliminate sod and weeds by smothering them with sheets of black plastic or sections of newspaper. Cover the garden plot entirely with plastic or newspaper, and anchor it with rocks. The grass or weeds should die in a few weeks; when dead, you can remove the plastic or newspaper and take away the dead grass and weeds. Persistent perennial weeds won't be killed easily, and you will have to remove them by hand. It's easiest to remove weeds when the soil is neither too wet and soggy nor too dry and hard.

Don't move on to Step Two ("Improving the Soil") until you feel confident that you've gotten rid of all the perennial weeds and every inch of their long roots. Remember, you will be going into the bed with your spade or a rototiller and chopping up the soil—this also chops up the weeds and encourages them to come back tenfold.

Step Two: Improving the Soil

Once you've removed the debris and vegetation, you can begin improving the soil by tilling it and adding amendments. When you till the soil you are breaking it up, providing aeration and improving its structure and drainage. A spade and fork are needed for this part of the process or try a power tiller, which is best for large areas that aren't too rocky. Rototillers, which you can rent at a local hardware store, aren't as useful in soils with large rocks, as the rotary blades won't operate properly.

A well-prepared bed will give you the best results, especially if you are planting perennials. Unlike annuals, which are short-lived plants with short roots, perennials can last years in the same location and develop long taproots that dig very deeply into the soil. Consider preparing your bed in one of the following three basic methods.

Simple Digging

In a simple-dug bed, you dig into the bed with your spade, turning over the soil with every spadeful. Just dig up a spadeful of soil and put it back in the hole so that the bottom layer of soil is now on top. As you dig, break up any large clumps of soil and remove debris as you find it. After you've dug the bed, add organic matter and blend it into the soil.

Single Digging

When you single dig the bed, you actually remove the soil and then return it or shift it to a different location. It's useful to have a large tarp or old sheet by the side of the bed for temporarily storing the soil. Start in a corner of the bed and work your way down the long end. Dig into the soil with your spade, taking up a spadeful (about 1 foot) of soil at a time. Place the soil on the tarp. Dig the length of the bed, creating a trench. Now use your fork to both break up the earth remaining in the trench and incorporate organic matter. After you've completed this task, start digging another strip beside the first. Remove the soil with your spade and turn it into the first trench. Take your fork and break up and amend the soil in the second trench. Go to the third strip and repeat the process. Continue doing this until you reach the other side of the bed; dig the last trench and add the soil from the first trench that you set aside on the tarp.

Double Digging

The procedure called double digging is a great deal of work, but it's the best way to provide your perennials with the nutrient-rich soil they need. When you double dig, you enrich and loosen the soil to a depth of 2 feet, giving deep-rooting perennials the aerated, nutritive soil they need. If your soil has drainage problems, double digging is probably your only answer.

It's best to do this job with a shovel and a fork. Divide your bed length-wise into foot-wide strips. Dig a 1-foot-wide trench with your shovel from one end of the bed to the other. Remove about 1 foot of topsoil from the trench and place it to the side of the garden bed. Add organic matter and other soil amendments to the trench and fork them into the subsoil on the

KEEPING COOL IN THE GARDEN

Avoid heat stress in the garden: Do the strenuous jobs, such as lifting and digging, in the morning; drink plenty of liquids, such as water, iced tea, and fruit juice; wear light-colored, lightweight clothes (including a hat); don't do too much too soon—gradually lengthen your exposure to the sun.

1. Using your shovel, dig a trench the entire width of the first foot-wide strip. Remove 1 foot of topsoil from the strip (making a trench) and place it to the side of the bed in a wheelbarrow or on a tarp.

2. Loosen the subsoil in the bottom of the trench with your spading fork. Add organic matter and other amendments to the subsoil in the bottom of the trench, mixing them in with your fork.

3. Make a second trench next to the first, spading the soil into the first trench. Repeat the procedure of loosening the subsoil and adding amendments with your spading fork. Continue through the width of the bed, trench by trench, until the whole bed has been dug.

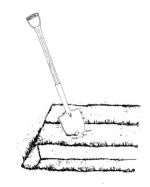

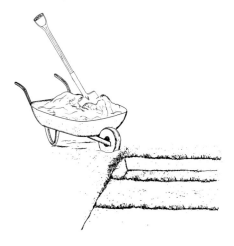

4. Add the soil from the first trench to fill the last week.

bottom of the trench. Try to incorporate the material as well as possible. Shovel the topsoil from the side of the bed back into the trench and add more organic matter, using your fork to incorporate it.

Make a second trench next to the first and do this procedure again. Dig out the topsoil and put it to the side of the bed, add organic matter to the subsoil in the trench, fork it in, replace the topsoil, and fork in more organic matter. Continue through the bed, trench by trench, until the whole bed has been dug.

Step Three: Raking the Soil

Finally, use your level-head rake to smooth and grade the soil. Break up any large clods of earth. Turn the rake around and use the flat surface of the rake to tamp down the soil. Water the newly prepared ground to help the soil settle.

THE GARDEN'S EDGE

After you've dug your garden bed, give it a clean edge with natural materials such as bricks or stones, or a synthetic material. The least expensive edging is the one you create yourself with an edger or a flat-edged spade.

You can create the most precise edge for a bed with the aid of sticks and strings. Or simply use your eye to determine a straight line. Either way, work down the length of the bed cutting into the sod about 3 inches deep with your edger or spade as you face the garden. If you use sticks and string, place sticks at the opposite ends of the bed, tie the string tautly across the sticks, and follow the line when you dig. For a curved bed, follow the outline as you would for a linear bed, making smaller cuts in the sod and overlapping where necessary to form the curve. Shake any loose topsoil from the sod into the garden bed and smooth it out.

Planting Perennials

Most home gardeners purchase perennials from a local nursery or mail-order catalog. You can also get your perennials free from gardening friends and neighbors, which may prove to be very good sources for new and interesting plants. However, be aware that these plants and soils may have pests and diseases you don't want imported to your garden.

Perennials in nurseries, available in containers, are usually sold in their second year and come in two-gallon pots. If you decide to get your plants from mail-order nurseries, they will probably arrive as bare-root perennials. These perennials are shipped when they're dormant; their bare roots are wrapped in shredded paper or peat moss. The brown tangle of roots can be a disappointing sight for the first-time gardener, but if a healthy bare-root perennial is planted properly, it will continue to grow into a healthy plant. They are just as viable as perennials grown in containers.

How can you tell if your perennial is healthy? Look it over at the nursery before you buy. Don't buy plants with leaves that are yellow or spotted or with leggy, wilted foliage. Avoid the plant if you see insects on it. Look at the bottom of the container to see if roots are coming through; if so, don't buy it. Chances are the plant is root bound, which means the roots have not grown properly because they have been constricted by the pot. Any perennials with broken branches or stems should be avoided. Finally, try to buy perennials that have not flowered. Since they flower for just a few weeks a year, you don't want to have to wait a whole year to enjoy the plant's flowers.

BUY EARLY FROM MAIL ORDER

Mail-order nurseries often have a wider selection of plants than your local nursery does, and you may find it easier to shop by mail. If you do so, follow these tips to get the best bare root plants for your money:

- Order early to be sure you get the selection you want.
- Look your bare-root perennials over carefully when they arrive, making sure the roots feel strong and plump, firm and pliable.
- If you receive a damaged plant, call the nursery grower immediately and ask to return the plant. Most growers have a reasonable return policy.
- Don't let the bare-root perennials dry out.

Best Times to Plant

The best time to plant perennials is on a cool, cloudy, windless day when the temperature is around 50°F. These conditions create the least amount of stress for the plants.

The best weather for planting is in the spring and fall. While most perennials can be planted in either season, fall planting is best for peonies, poppies, and bearded irises, three perennials whose root systems start to develop early in the spring. Any perennials planted in the fall need to be put in early enough in the season to allow time for their root systems to develop. Plants not firmly anchored into the soil can heave out of the ground as a result of ground freezing and thawing.

Spring planting is usually the best time to plant in areas where winters are cold because plants' roots have time to settle into the cool soil before the summer heat arrives. Avoid planting too early in the spring, however, when the soil is still wet and frigid. Root growth will be hampered by soil that is too cold.

Spacing Perennials

Perennials need 1 to 2 feet of space between them. The tallest ones, such as goatsbeard (*Aruncus dioicus*), will need more space. If you plant them too closely together, you will have to move them when they outgrow their spaces. The healthiest, most disease-resistant perennials are those that are spaced properly. Spacing requirements accompany cultural and planting instructions. Look in the appendix for the spacing requirements for the perennials mentioned in this book.

Planting Nursery-Grown Perennials

Perennials should be planted at the same depth they were in their containers. Use a trowel or a spade to dig the hole, depending on the size of the perennial.

Soak perennials in containers for a few hours before planting. This will cause the roots and stems to become turgid.

Dig a hole that is wider and deeper than the root mass of the perennial. Place soil amendments on the bottom of the hole and refill the hole about

Take care when spacing perennials. Here are some tips:

- Always leave 1 foot between any structure (a house, for instance) and the back of the garden.
- Be careful when planting near trees, and avoid planting near shallow-rooted trees, such as maple.
- To help you space properly, measure out every foot in your garden, dividing the bed into square feet. Draw a line with a stick or use lime, if you have it, and plant perennials at the recommended spacing.
- Plant annuals to fill in the empty spaces—at the end of the season, you will be amazed by how much your perennials have grown.

halfway with the soil you just removed. Tip the plant out of the pot and into your hand and gently place it in the hole. Press the soil in and around the plant to remove air pockets; you can use your heel to tamp in the soil around larger plants. This will ensure that the roots make contact with the soil. Water well and place the plant label nearby. When you've planted the entire bed, give all the plants a good, deep soak.

Planting Bare-Root Perennials

Before you plant your bare-root perennials, soak the roots in a bucket of luke-warm water for six to twelve hours. This will give the roots a chance to become turgid, or swollen. Dig a hole twice the size of the root mass and add organic matter to the soil. Mix it with soil, making a small mound on the bottom of the hole. Place the roots on the mound and spread them out. Make sure the crown (where the root mass and stems meet) is at ground level. Fill the hole with the remaining soil and tamp it down to remove air pockets. Water thoroughly.

Planting Perennials in Containers

Perennials planted in containers should be treated differently from those that are planted in the ground. Container plants will probably need more frequent

The day before you plant:

- Check your garden plan; make last minute changes.

The day you plant:

- Bring your spade, shovel, shears, gardening bag or wheelbarrow, level-head rake or lawn rake, labels and pen, hose or watering can with you to the garden.
- Give your plants the best start possible. If container-grown stock is pot-bound, loosen the roots to encourage new growth by gently disentangling them with your fingers. Scratch at the roots to break up the root ball.
- Don't let your plants sit in the hot sun while you prepare the soil. Keep them in a shady area.
- Keep the ground moist after planting!

waterings than garden plants. Also, since the container may be the plant's home for many years, make sure it is large enough to accommodate the perennial as it grows to its full size. Check the "Plant Portraits" in Part Four for the specific needs of your perennial. Perennials that develop long taproots will do best in deep containers, and perennials that require heavy feeding, such as phlox (*Phlox paniculata*), will benefit from a rich soil.

A good potting soil for perennials in containers is two parts topsoil, one part peat moss, and one part perlite. Soil for heavy feeders, such as phlox, should also get plenty of organic matter blended into the soil. Add a few handfuls of compost to the soil. If you decide to use a soilless potting medium from a nursery, you may need to fertilize your perennials with liquid or dry fertilizer, since the mix won't have any nutritional value.

Moisten the soil before putting it in the container. Let it sit for about a half hour to give it time to settle and allow the air bubbles to escape, then add it to the container. Place your plants in the container, moving them around to get the desired look. Don't be too quick to plant them. Take a few minutes to decide where the plants look best. Remember to give your perennials adequate spacing. Plant perennials to the same depth they were in their original containers, being sure the roots do not extend out of the soil, exposed to the drying effects of wind and sun.

The technique for planting bare-root perennials in containers is the same as for planting them in the ground. Make a small mound in the bottom of the container and spread the roots out.

Large containers (more than 3 feet wide) should be elevated on bricks or two-by-fours to improve drainage and air circulation.

Perennial plants eventually outgrow their original containers and will need to be repotted every few years into larger containers. Some plants, however, such as blue African lily (*Agapanthus africanus*) actually prefer to be pot-bound (see Part Four, page 106). Repot your perennials if you see roots coming through the bottom of the pot, and take the time to clean the old, empty container with a 10-percent bleach solution before storing or reusing it later. Add fresh, moistened potting mix to the new, larger container and replant. (If the perennial has become severely potbound—with the roots winding around the root ball—take a sharp knife and slice the roots off on the sides and bottom. Cutting the roots will allow them to grow more freely in the new container.) Tamp down and water thoroughly.

As noted, perennials in containers may need to be watered more frequently than their counterparts in the ground, simply because their roots can't dig deep into the soil for necessary water. Thus the container's size, placement, and material, as well as the soil you provide, all influence how much water you will need to give your plants.

The Ensuing Days in Beds and Containers

Watch your newly planted perennials closely. Check them every day for the first week or so after planting: Make sure the soil is firm around the plant and evenly moist. If it feels dry to the touch, water. As the ground settles around the plant, make sure the roots are not exposed and that it is planted at the right depth. If you think the perennial wasn't planted deeply enough, simply take it out of the hole and replant at the correct depth.

Skills in the Garden: Watering, Feeding, Weeding

In this section and the next you will learn all about watering, feeding, weeding, staking, deadheading, dividing—everything you need to know to keep your perennials healthy and producing beautiful flowers.

Watering Basics

As you learned in Part One, climate and soil type influence how much water you need to give your plants and how much water will be retained in the soil. Because sandy soils dry out more quickly than clay, they need to be watered more frequently than clay and even loamy soils. Gardens in hot climates need more water than those in cooler climates.

The most important rule in watering plants is to water deeply. This encourages the plant to dig deeply into the soil, thus creating healthier roots: If you just sprinkle water on the soil the water will not penetrate and the plant will be forced to establish roots where the water is—close to the surface. This kind of shallow watering will actually do more harm than good. A plant with deep roots will survive drought and other stressful conditions.

To give your plant deep waterings, let the water run out of your hose at a fairly slow rate. An hour or so after watering test how far the water has penetrated the soil. If it feels dry 1 to 2 inches below the surface, you need to provide more water. Finally, it's always best to water in the mornings or evenings, when the temperature drops. Try not to water in the middle of the day.

Check the soil's water content with a small hand tool, such as a trowel. Stick it in 1 to 2 inches and loosen the soil: If the soil appears moist, don't

---

WATERING BASICS

Learn the signs of a plant in need of water:

- Wilted stem
- Dropping foliage
- Dropping buds
- Yellowing or browning leaves
- Dry soil

water; if it's dry, and rain is not in the forecast, water. Your plants will need at least 1 inch of water a week, whether you provide it or the environment does. Perennials need water during their growing seasons and may need to be watered while dormant in the winter months in certain regions of the country. If the soil is dry and not frozen, it's a good idea to water.

Watering systems such as drip irrigation and soaker hoses can work wonders in areas where rainfall is limited. Look into watering systems with automatic timers if you can't water your perennials on a regular schedule.

Fertilizing Perennials

If you've taken the time to prepare your perennial bed well, the good, loamy soil will provide your perennials with just about all the nutrients they need. Keep the soil replenished by spreading about 2 to 3 inches of organic matter over the bed each spring. Incorporate the organic matter into the top layer of soil and spread it around plants. It's also a good idea to sprinkle a dry balanced fertilizer (10–10–10) around the plants early in the spring for added nutrients.

Weeding

Weeds are unwelcome visitors in our gardens because they compete for water, nutrients, and sunlight—and usually win. They are, in the most generous sense, simply unwanted plants, whether annuals, biennials, or perennials. Perennial weeds, such as dandelions, will return unless you remove the entire root system. Annual weeds are also a nuisance; they come back year after year with every new crop of seeds. It's always best to eliminate weeds when they are still young, before they either grow strong roots (in the case of perennials) or go to seed (in the case of annuals).

One of the best ways to identify weeds in your area is with the help of an identification book that will teach you how different weeds grow and how to get rid of them. You'll know whether you're digging up a wild carrot with a long taproot or a creeping buttercup, which grows by runners. Runners, or "stolons" are roots that extend along the surface of the soil horizontally, rooting themselves as they spread. Or you may find your region has a lot of dock, a weed that grows by seeds.

You'll see many products for removing weeds on the market; these are known as herbicides. Herbicides kill plants by starving them to death. Remember, however, these plant killers are nonselective: They kill *all* vegetation. Certainly, they aren't meant for the garden, and they aren't a good idea anywhere else, particularly because of their harmful effects on animal life, water, and other aspects of the environment. If a weed is harmful to you or your family, such as poison ivy, use a weed killer and follow the instructions carefully to remove the weed. Use caution when using herbicides, and don't use them at all if children or pets are present.

Hoeing, Hand-Pulling, and Mulching

Weeds can be dug out with the help of a tool known as a cultivator, or hoe. Take a wheelbarrow or an old sheet with you into the garden to lay the weeds on as you pull them up. Be sure to dig up all of the weed; even a small piece of a weed's root left in the ground will later emerge as a plant, so carefully sift through the soil to extricate each piece you find.

Toss the weeds into the compost bin if you have one. Don't let them lie around on the ground as they may sow themselves back into the soil, creating yet more work. You'll quickly learn that weeds are nothing if not tenacious and persistent—get rid of them!

Mulching

Use a mulch to control weeds. Mulches not only stifle the growth of weeds but organic mulches will improve the texture and tilth of the soil. Mulches will keep the soil from getting too hot in the summer and help it remain at an even temperature.

The mulch you choose should improve the look of your garden. Mulches are different colors, shapes, and sizes, from very light, disk-shaped hulls of buckwheat to coarse, nugget-like bark chips. Bark chips are fine in large shrub borders but not as appropriate in a perennial bed with smaller plants. The big rough nuggets detract from the delicacy of the flowers. Some of the prettiest mulches can also be expensive, but one of the best organic mulches for the perennial bed is simply compost, which is free if you make it yourself. Use your taste in determining which mulch to lay on your bed.

Add a layer of mulch to a well-weeded garden in the late spring. Make sure your young plants are not buried under mulch.

Perennial Care: Staking, Deadheading, Dividing, Fall Cleanup, Winter Mulches

Many perennials need to be deadheaded after their flowers have bloomed, pinched to promote a nice, bushy shape, or staked to keep the stems from falling over. These are the routine chores you can expect to perform for many perennials, and they are very easy to do once you've got the hang of it. As you get to know your perennials, you will begin to recognize when various chores need to be done and for which plants (when you see your peonies flopping about you will think, "Yes, they need that peony ring!").

It's best to go into the garden armed with shears and a bucket. Deadhead where necessary and examine your plants for signs of any potential problems. Cut off or remove any dead or broken branches. It's an opportunity to see your plants up close and maybe even discover some new flower buds.

Staking

Staking is important for plants that need some support to help them stay upright. You can buy stakes to fit your needs at your local garden center. Different types of plants require different types of stakes. For instance, peonies (*Paeonia lactiflora*) need to be staked with a "peony ring," which is a metal ring with wire legs (often coated with a green paint) that encircles the plant, keeping its heavy flowers from toppling the plant over. Baby's breath (*Gypsophila paniculata*) often needs staking to keep its multiple, billowy stems from falling over. You can make your own hooplike structure for baby's breath with a few strong stakes and string. Place the stakes around the plant and run the string from stake to stake. Tall, single-stemmed plants benefit from bamboo stakes, which are relatively inexpensive. Loop a piece of twine around both the stem and the bamboo. Try not to let the plant touch the stake.

Always try to place the stakes so that they're hidden, if possible. Peony rings are fairly impossible to conceal; but other stakes, such as bamboo, can be hidden by foliage.

Finally, you can also plant strong plants beside those that flop. For instance, a yucca plant (*Yucca filamentosa*) can be used to support a plant that

THE BEST MULCHES

Here is a list of natural mulches. Choose a mulch that will suit your specific needs. Most mulches can be purchased at your local garden center or found around the house or yard.

Mulch	Description
Buckwheat hulls	Tiny, dark brown, lightweight, disk-shaped hulls; expensive; retains moisture well
Cocoa shells	Rich brown color; chocolate aroma that disappears quickly; expensive
Compost	Natural looking; water retentive; free if you make it yourself; can be purchased from the nursery
Evergreen boughs	Good winter mulch; easily available from prunings of evergreen trees or Christmas decorations
Grass clippings	Free; decompose quickly, making them a good mulch choice
Leaf mold	Made of rotted leaves; one of the best mulches; full of nutrients; will break down and improve the structure of your soil; soft brown color looks natural; available free by making your own or from your community
Leaves, chopped or shredded	One of the best mulches for adding nutrients and structure to the soil; make by running your lawn mower back and forth over the leaves until they are chopped
Peat moss	Not recommended as a mulch
Pine needles	Light and airy; look natural; easy to collect if you have pine trees
Salt hay	Made of dried salt marsh grasses; available in coastal parts of the country; more expensive than straw, but it is seed-free
Sawdust	Not recommended; free or inexpensive
Stones (pebbles, gravel)	Can be very attractive, particularly in an Asian garden design; natural looking
Straw (hay)	Not recommended as mulch; easily available
Tree bark	Commercially available as chips, shredded, and ground; shredded bark is one of the most commonly used mulches and is available in coarse and fine grades; very attractive

Spread 2–4 inches on a level bed; can easily be blown away in very windy areas

Spread 3–4 inches on a level bed; don't use on slopes where it may wash off; too much moisture may cause mildew and mushrooms to sprout

Spread 3–4 inches on garden beds; may contain weed seeds

Place one or more layers of evergreen boughs over and around tender plants in the winter after the ground has frozen; in the spring, remove the layers slowly over a period of weeks; good for erosion control; not recommended for summer, since dry boughs can be a fire hazard

Spread 2 inches on garden beds; use only when dry, since wet clippings can breed flies; dry a day or two before using; may contain weed seeds

Spread 3–4 inches on garden beds

Spread 4–6 inches on garden beds; don't use whole leaves, as they will mat and trap excess moisture

Use only as a soil conditioner; used as a mulch, it prevents water from passing through to the soil beneath

Spread 3 inches around acid-loving plants; useful on slopes; refreshen often, since dry pine needles can be a fire hazard; highly acidic

Spread 3–4 inches around plants; good winter mulch for tender perennials and bulbs

Unattractive; can be a fire hazard

Spread 1 inch around the garden bed, being careful not to set any too close to plants' stems; very useful in desert plantings; safe for arid regions subject to wildfires; does not add nutrients to the garden

Use on pathways to keep weeds down; best when well rotted; don't use in gardens because it contains weed seeds; look for weed-free straw

Spread 2–3 inches on garden beds; chips are better suited for larger plants, such as those in a shrub border; if you have the space to store it, purchase bark by the truckload and apply it to garden beds throughout the summer

may flop, such as baby's breath. (These plants also make a striking plant combination.) Plant them next to each other, at their right spacing distances.

Staked plants

Ringed plants

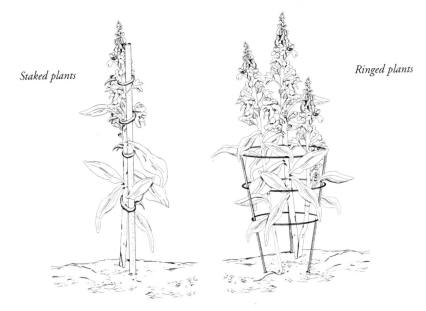

Deadheading

Deadheading is a technique for removing flowers that have faded and preventing the plant from setting seeds. It also neatens up the appearance of the plant and often encourages it to bloom longer. When you see a faded or brown blossom, remove the flower with your fingers or scissors. For purely aesthetic reasons, you may want to cut the flower to the base if there are no flowers or leaves on the stem or, if there are leaves, to the next set of leaves.

When you see a faded or brown blossom, remove the flower with your fingers or scissors.

Pinching

Pinching is a method of pruning seedlings to create a fuller plant with more stems and flowers. When plants are young, use your fingertips (or scissors) to snip off the stems' growing tips back to the closest set of leaves. Not all perennials need pinching back, but those that do, such as garden mums (*Dendranthema* × *grandiflora*), will benefit from this technique greatly. Gardeners in the South can also pinch plants in the aster family to prolong flowering. Northern gardeners shouldn't pinch these plants, as they will flower too late in the season and perhaps be lost to a fall frost. Be sure to read Part Four to find out about which plants need pinching and deadheading.

Prune your plants to keep them growing compactly and to encourage fullness.

Dividing

Every couple of years your perennials will need to be divided. They should be divided and replanted in the spring or fall, when the soil temperature is cool. The general rule of thumb is perennials that bloom in the spring or summer should be divided in fall and perennials that bloom in the fall should

Autumn in the Garden

Finally, in the fall, your perennial garden needs to be cleaned up. This is the time to rake leaves out of the bed and cut back perennials. Fall is a great time in the garden; the days are cooler and dryer, renewing your energy. It's also the perfect time to plant more perennials and order catalogs from seed and nursery companies to read throughout the winter for inspiration.

When the leaves change color, the perennials in your garden will begin to look as though they were dying: They will turn brown and the stems will fall over. This is natural. Your perennials are dying back. When this begins to happen, cut back the foliage to 6 inches from the ground. This is one of the most important chores in the fall garden. The other important fall chore is removing leaves as they fall to the ground. An accumulation of big, wet leaves can create a home for rodents and increase the possibility of diseases in the garden.

GARDENERS WITH PERENNIALS IN CONTAINERS

Gardeners with perennials in containers should also cut back perennials in the fall and remove any leaves that accumulate in the container. Containers can also be moved to a sheltered position, perhaps near a south-facing wall, and mulched with evergreen boughs in cold climates.

Cutting back perennials neatens up the appearance of the plant and the garden. On the other hand, some perennials—for example, astilbe (*Astilbe* × *arendsii*) and some sedums—look good all winter when their flowers are left to turn deep bronze or gold. So to keep your garden interesting through the winter, you won't want to cut back these perennials. See Part Four for specifics about which perennials to cut back.

Winter Mulches

Your new plants need to be protected with a winter mulch, and perennials that are marginally hardy in your area need winter protection every year. Apply a winter mulch when the ground is frozen to keep plants at an even temperature (see "The Best Mulches," pages 80–81). After the snow has settled, add winter boughs to keep the snow in place.

Snow, often referred to as "the poor man's mulch," will insulate your plants, will keep plants from heaving out of the ground before they have properly rooted, and will keep roots from drying out. In fact, a good solid blanket of snow can be the best thing for a plant.

In the spring, remove the mulch gradually over a period of weeks. Take it off the garden bed first, and remove it from the crowns of plants last. This way, if there are any late frosts the plants won't be exposed. Add your winter mulches to the compost heap and cut back any perennials that were left standing over the winter, taking care not to damage any young shoots.

The Natural Way to Healthy Plants

The first step to dealing with a damaged plants is to correctly diagnose the problem. Usually we have only the damaged plant as evidence of a problem: We often don't see the insects nibbling away, and we find out about the diseases afflicting our plants only when the symptoms appear.

It's important first to consider every possible reason for the damage we see and to rule out factors such as underwatering, overwatering, sun scorch, wind, and other climatic factors. The evidence—wilted leaves, for instance— notifies us of the need to investigate further. It's best to identify the culprit and remedy the problem before it gets out of hand. However, a munched leaf here or a wilted leaf there is no cause for alarm. Take a reasonable approach to dealing with pests and insects in the garden. Don't reach for chemicals: We have learned the hard way how devastating harsh pesticides are on the environment.

Common Diseases

In this section you'll learn about the symptoms of diseases and various remedies. Plant diseases are easier to understand if we think about them the way we think about our own illnesses—they are classified similarly. We get fevers and blisters which can be symptoms of a cold; plants get wilts, blights, and rusts, which are the names of the visible symptoms for their ailments.

Today many gardeners favor the use of integrated pest management (IPM) when dealing with insects and diseases. This is really just a new name for an old practice, and one that makes a lot of sense.

The goal of IPM is to use biological and cultural remedies before resorting to the prudent use of pesticides. The IPM program is built around the use of pest-resistant plants and shrubs, good maintenance of those plants, and careful monitoring of plants before pest and disease problems arise.

The building blocks of IPM are as follows:

1. Don't create problems in your garden. Take steps to avoid "bad" gardening habits, such as overwatering, overfeeding, and crowding plants, that can result in encouraging pests to gather and reproduce in your garden.
2. Select plants, flowers, trees, and shrubs with care. Use plant varieties that are proven to withstand insects. Some plants are not as attractive to pests as other plants are; check with your nursery or garden center to find out which plants are the most pest-proof for your location.
3. Examine plants routinely and carefully. It's very important that you learn to identify insects and diseases when they first appear. It may not be easy at first, if you can't tell a good bug from a bad one, but you can begin to learn which ones are harmful and should be controlled.
4. Use natural predators, such as ladybug beetles, green lacewings, and earwigs.
5. As a last resort only, use an appropriate pesticide.

Plant diseases can be caused by a virus, bacterium, or fungus. Fungal diseases tend to be the most common and are most likely to occur when growing conditions for the plant are either too wet or too dry. Viruses are the most destructive to plants, and once they infect a plant there is little that can be done to restore it.

Some common plant diseases you may see are described below.

Blight

Blight is a fungal disease that appears as a grayish powder on buds and flowers. Plants wilt, then die. It can be a problem when humidity is high. Remove and discard all infected plants.

Fusarium Wilt

Fusarium wilt is a fungal disease that causes leaves and stems to wilt, turn yellow, then die. Often the symptoms of fusarium wilt appear only on one side of the plant. Remove and destroy infected plants.

Leaf Spot

Leaf spot is caused by various fungi and bacteria and appear as white, brown, yellow, or black circles. The best way to prevent leaf spot is to maintain good air circulation between plants. Discard the diseased foliage to control its spread.

Mosaic

Mosaic is caused by viruses (each strain of mosaic virus is specific to a plant or family) and the symptoms are yellow and green mottled or streaked leaves, stems, and flowers. Dig up the plant and throw it away.

Leaf spot   *Powdery mildew*

Powdery Mildew

Powdery mildew is a fungus that appears as a gray or white powdery substance on foliage and stems. It is most often a problem toward the end of summer when humidity is high and nights begin to cool. To prevent powdery mildew, plant cultivars in your area that are not susceptible to this disease, do not overcrowd plants, and give your plants good air circulation. As a last resort, use horticultural oil according to the manufacturer's directions. Remove and destroy any infected parts of the plants.

Rust

Rust is a fungus that appears as powdery orange or brown spots on foliage, especially on the undersides of leaves. Cut off the diseased portions of the plant and spray the remaining plant with a fungicide.

When Insects Come

When the bugs come—and they will—be prepared! Learn to distinguish between helpful and destructive insects. Be aware of unhealthy symptoms in your plants (often the only evidence of an insect infestation). The next section addresses various methods by which you can eliminate pests.

Inspect plants as often as possible, checking tops and undersides of leaves, stems, buds and flowers, and bases. Note all leaves that are partially eaten, covered with webbing, or a different color. Look for blackened, wilted, or chewed stems, sticky substances, or discolored flower buds. You should also look for clues in the surrounding soil surface, such as loose soil mounds.

Physical Controls

Physical control is the most preferable means of eliminating insects in the garden and also the most hands-on approach to getting rid of them. You can hand pick many insects, including aphids, slugs, and Japanese beetles, removing them from the plants as you find them and crushing them or depositing them in a plastic bag. You may wish to wear gloves to avoid an allergic reaction. If enough insects are hand picked in the spring and early summer, succeeding generations may be severely reduced.

Some pests can be identified by the type of damage they do your plants.

- Leaves with holes: Caterpillars, grasshoppers, and beetles leave a kind of leaf skeleton and may chew away the surface leaf tissue.
- Seedlings cut off at ground level: Cutworms.
- White pathways on leaves: Leaf miners.
- Oozing, sticky sap: Borers burrow into stems and branches, leaving oozing, sticky sap or sawdust.
- Wilted, twisted, yellow, spotted, or curled leaves: Aphids, mealy bugs, scale, and whiteflies suck the sap from plants.
- Sticky, shiny substance, called honeydew, on the leaf surface: Aphids or scale.

Another physical control is a strong spray of water aimed at an insect. This is effective for removing aphids and other small insects.

Biological Controls

Natural predators of harmful insects are extremely useful in any garden. Many beneficial insects can be purchased in egg form from mail-order catalogs and released into your garden. Or you can attract them to your yard by growing the plants they like. Many of them are lured to flowers with an umbel shape, such as Queen Anne's lace and dill, which allows them to get into the nectar easily. Garlic chives

Green lacewing

and all members of the mint family are also attractive to ladybug beetles. Other plants beneficial insects tend to be attracted to are cosmos, sweet alyssum, and chamomile.

Other biological controls include the use of microorganisms, such as the bacterium *Bacillus thuringiensis* (BT; sold under the trade names Thuricide and Dipel). BT kills caterpillars and their larvae by paralyzing their intestinal tracts. It is applied as a liquid spray or in granular form. Milky spore disease

OUR ALLIES IN THE GARDEN

Nobody wants to eliminate destructive pests from the garden more than the gardener, right? Wrong. Voracious insects, such as those listed here, along with bats, reptiles, and other predatory creatures have the same desire (albeit

Garden Allies	Characteristics
Bugs	Assassin bugs, big-eyed bugs, and damsel bugs; about $1/2$ inch long; among the most effective predators
Dragonflies	Pretty as they are useful
Earthworms	Beneficial because their digestive activities increase available phosphorus and potassium in the soil; they are almost always a sign of healthy, biologically active soil with good structure
Fireflies	Inhabit open areas where the grass is tall.
Green lacewings	Delicate; bright green with lacy green wings; adults and larvae are voracious predators of aphids; sometimes referred to as aphid lions (although the larvae look like little grayish alligators)
Ground beetles	Range in size from $1/8$ to 1 inch long; most are black, but some blue-black or green; night feeders
Ladybugs (ladybug beetles)	The most beloved of beneficial insects need no description; partial to warm, sunny gardens; will fly away if they aren't happy
Parasitic wasps	Nonstinging, tiny wasps that lay eggs in other pests' eggs; types include chalcids, ichneumons, and trichogrammas
Praying mantises	One of the most voracious insects; eat anything and everything; not recommended
Robber flies	About 1 inch long with large heads and slender abdomens; they like sunny, open fields and pastures
Spiders	Voracious consumers; some are deadly (the black widow and the brown violin) most are just annoying; types useful in the garden are daddy longlegs, jumping, and crab
Tachinid flies	Adults look like large houseflies; frequently seen flying around plants or on the ground; lay their eggs on other insects

they desire the pests for dinner) and can be extremely helpful in controlling the pest populations.

Pests They Pray On	Where You'll Find Them
Aphids; leafhoppers; small caterpillars; spider mites	Nature
Mosquitoes; midges; gnats	Nature
None	Nature; mail-order nurseries
Larvae of pest insects; slugs; snails	Nature; keep grass on the tall side to encourage them
Soft-bodied insects such as aphids; thrips; whiteflies; small worms; scale insects; eggs of other insects	Nature; eggs are available from mail-order catalogs; 1,000 eggs are enough for 500 square feet of garden
Cutworms; snails; slugs and their eggs; tent caterpillars	Nature
Aphids (one of the best biological controls); leaf miners' eggs; scale; spider mites; root worms; weevil	Nature; live insects are available from mail-order nurseries
Become parasites of whiteflies, cutworms, aphids, caterpillars, moths, and other pests	Nature; available from mail-order nurseries; 5,000 wasps are enough for a large garden.
Everything, including your plants; indiscriminate feeders	Nature; egg cases are available from mail-order nurseries
Horseflies; bees; beetles; butterflies; moths; leafhoppers	Nature
All pest insects; indiscriminate feeders	Nature
Become parasites of cutworms, beetle larvae, caterpillars	Nature

contains *Bacillus popillae,* which is used to control Japanese beetle larvae and other grubs. Japanese beetles begin in the soil as grubs, and when milky spore disease is applied to the lawn in the spring or fall it eliminates the grubs from the soil. The process may take a few years. Another pathogen is nuclear polydedrons virus (NPV), which is used to control gypsy moth caterpillars. These and other microbial control agents are commercially available. They are all selective and harmless to good insects.

Finally, natural predators found around the garden—such as toads, bats, birds, lizards, snakes, and salamanders—are all happy to assist you in biologically controlling pests. They should be welcomed visitors to your garden.

Chemical Controls

The third method for suppressing pests and disease is chemical control. This approach should be used only in cases of extreme infestation.

There are some chemical controls that are acceptable even in the organic garden, such as dishwashing liquid diluted in water and home-made sprays made with onion, garlic, and hot peppers, which are used to control soft-bodied pests such as aphids, spider mites, and whiteflies. A soap mixture will get rid of leaf miners and Japanese beetles, among other insects—but use only in cases of severe infestation.

Here are some of the most troublesome garden pests you may encounter along with ways to control them.

Aphids

Aphids are small, soft-bodied, pear-shaped bugs with or without wings, black, green, or gold in color. They suck the juices from stems, leaves, and flower buds and tend to go after new growth. The result is wilted or malformed leaves. They reproduce often, so early detection can be critical in controlling them.

A strong spray of water from a hose is usually the best way to get rid of aphids. You can also control infestations by picking them off or removing and destroying the leaves with aphids. Ladybug beetles and their larvae, lacewings and their larvae,

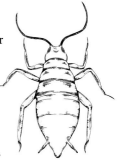

Aphid

and syrphid flies all eat aphids. As a last resort, spray them with a mixture of dishwashing soap and water.

Caterpillars

Caterpillars can devastate foliage, and some caterpillars, known as corn and stalk borers, tunnel into the stems of many annuals and do a great deal of damage.

It's best to remove caterpillars by hand picking as soon as they appear. You can also use the microbial insecticide called BT to get rid of them.

Cutworms

Cutworms attack young plants, chewing their stems at the base and causing them to fall over. If you have a cutworm problem, affix a plastic or cardboard collar around the base of your plants to protect them.

Cutworm

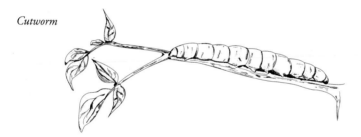

Fire Ants

Fire ants are common in many parts of the United States, from North Carolina to California and throughout the Southwest. They are approximately $1/4$ inch long and are yellow, reddish brown, or black. Queens (which live five to seven years!) and reproductive males have wings and are larger than the wingless worker ants. They chew on seeds.

Pour hot water on the mound to kill the ants inside. It's best to pour the water in the morning when the ants are near the top of the mound, but avoid stepping on the mound. If that doesn't work, use a very weak solution of boric acid on cotton balls: Mix 1 teaspoon boric acid, 4 tablespoons sugar, and 2 cups water. Soak the cotton balls and place them in jar. Leave the jar open and place it on its side near the mound.

Japanese Beetles

Adult beetles have metallic blue or green bodies and copper-colored wings. They begin in their larval stages as white grubs in the lawn. The first step in controlling Japanese beetles is to get rid of white grubs by applying milky spore disease to lawns and grassy areas. Hand pick the adults. In severe cases, make a mix of equal parts water and dishwashing liquid and spray it on the plants.

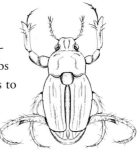

Japanese beetle

Leaf Miners

Leaf miners are green or black insects that grow to $1/8$ inch. They tunnel between the upper and lower leaf surface, leaving a white trail behind them.

The best way to get rid of leaf miners is with biological controls, such as ladybugs and lacewings, which eat the eggs of leaf miners. Remove and destroy the infested leaves.

Nematodes

Nematodes are microscopic, wormlike insects (but are not related to worms); although many are harmful, some are beneficial in the garden. The harmful nematodes can cause a variety of damage, including burrowing into plant tissue. Nematode damage is evident by lesions and swollen roots and by yellow or wilted foliage.

The best way to prevent nematodes is by planting nematode-resistant varieties and keeping the garden bed clean. If you do get nematodes, get rid of the plants. Don't plant in the same spot the following year.

Spider Mites

Spider mites are arachnids, not insects. These tiny, orange, brown, or green mites suck juices from plants, turning leaves yellow, silver, or speckled. Regular hosing can help a spider mite infestation, as will importing ladybug beetles and lacewings. As a last resort, spray the plant with insecticidal soap, lime spray, or a combination of both.

Spider mites

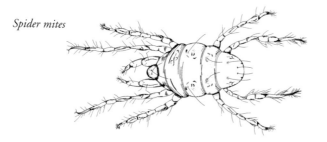

Thrips

Thrips are a family of tiny yellow or black flies. The telltale sign that a plant has been attacked by thrips is a silvery area on the damaged leaves and wilting. Thrips thrive on plants that are under stress, sucking fluids from leaves.

The remedies for thrips are similar to those for spider mites. Hosing with water will help, as will releasing the adults and larvae of ladybug beetles and/or lacewing larvae. As a last resort, spray the plants with insecticidal soap in the early morning when thrips are least active.

Small and Large Animals

Small animal, small problem; big animal, big problem—right? Unfortunately, this isn't true. One of the biggest problems in the garden is one of the smallest members of the animal kingdom: slugs, which are part of the mollusk family. But then birds eat seeds, deer eat tulips, and moles dig holes. While all of these creatures can act destructively at times, in the end they are no more than unwanted animals in your garden. Remember that the garden is your ecosystem, and you need to keep the system balanced. Don't be quick to use any harmful or cruel methods of eliminating unwanted animals from your garden.

Here are some of the most common unwanted animals and some humane ways to get deal with them.

Deer

Deer are most effectively kept from gardens with electronic fencing, but they may be deterred by hanging Irish Spring brand soap from the plants. You can also try Milorganite, which is sewage sludge; reapply it to the soil after each rain, as it will wash away. This can be effective when properly used, but if you have a lot of deer you're going to have a lot of deer problems.

OUTSMARTING THE DEER

A few perennials the deer don't like:

Astilbe (*Astilbe × arendsii*)
Boltonia (*Boltonia asteroides*)
Butterfly weed (*Asclepias tuberosa*)
Columbine (*Aquilegia* spp.)
Cranesbill (*Geranium* spp.)

Japanese anemone (*Anemone × hybrida*)
Sneezeweed (*Helenium autumnale*)
Threadleaf coreopsis (*Coreopsis verticillata*)

Moles and Voles

If moles and voles are your marauders, try to get rid of the destructive tunnels they create throughout your lawn and garden by putting mothballs in the tunnels—they hate the smell. Or soak the soil around mole tunnels and mounds with castor oil, which they also dislike. Mix it with water in a 50:50 ratio and use it year-round directly on the mole holes and tunnels or to create a barrier around your garden. It stays effective for about two months.

Rabbits

If rabbits are feasting on your favorite plants, try planting the perennials among the foods rabbits hate, such as plants in the onion family. This will keep the rabbits away from the plants they like. Fox oil, also known as stink oil and bone oil, is an organic product that is said to deter rabbits with its pungent odor. You can pick it up in the pharmacy. Mix the oil with water and sprinkle it on the soil.

Snails and Slugs

The most effective solution for getting rid of snails and slugs is diatomaceous earth (DE) This is an abrasive powder made from the finely ground remains of single-cell aquatic plants. Dust it on the edges of your garden bed to keep the mollusks away. DE kills the snails and slugs by dehydrating them when they crawl over it. Or try burying a dish (a empty cat food or tuna can also works well) of beer in the garden, buried up to soil level. They are attracted to the fermented smell, fall in, and drown.

The best way to keep your garden free of slugs and snails is to keep your garden free of debris. You can also search for slugs and snails at night and remove them by hand when you find them.

the burpee basics'

guide to

perennials

The Essentials

- Choosing the Right Perennials
- Plant Portraits

Choosing the Right Perennials

In the next section you'll find detailed descriptions of seventy-five popular perennials, including information about each plant's size, flower color, and maintenance requirements. All of the plants are easy to find in garden centers and from mail-order nurseries. As you learn more about these plants, you will discover which ones are right for you. The amount of sun your garden receives, the condition of your soil, and your local climate all have an effect on which perennials will thrive in your yard.

Right Zone, Right Soil

In choosing perennials, your first consideration should be the plant's hardiness and whether your climatic region is suitable for the plant. First find out what your hardiness zone is by looking at the USDA Hardiness Zone Map, on page 166; then check each plant's hardiness zone (listed in the "Plant Portraits") to see if it will do well in your area. Unless you can provide a perennial with the right climatic conditions, you will probably fight a losing battle—the plant will eventually succumb to either winter cold or summer heat. Perennials that are adaptable to your environment are relatively easy to maintain.

Another important factor is your soil. Always plant perennials in the type of soil they require. Just about every plant needs a soil that is well draining, or does not hold too much water. Although established perennials have particular water needs (some need more than others), all new transplants need plenty of deep soakings to help them establish deep root systems. Once the plants are established, continue to water them throughout the growing season according to their needs. Perennials that prefer conditions on the dry side will need to be watered only when it is very hot. Perennials that prefer moist conditions should be planted where they will get water easily from the ground, either in a bog or near a river or pond. If nature can't provide your plants with what they need, you will have to.

Finally, consider a plant's sun and shade requirements. Some plants require full sun, others partial shade, and others full shade. For more information refer to "The Sun," on page 6.

Rating Perennials

Some perennials are low maintenance, trouble free, and require little from the gardener; whereas others demand more maintenance. Try to figure out how much time you want to spend tending the garden, and then decide which plants you want to use based on your own needs. For instance, sedum and hostas are relatively undemanding, as are purple coneflower and rudbeckia.

To help you make an informed decision, the plants listed here have been divided into three categories, indicated by trowels (🛠). The easiest plants have been awarded one trowel. These plants, such as hostas, coreopsis, sedum, and yucca, require the least attention and fuss. They tend to be easy to grow because they aren't very particular.

Plants rated as two trowels are perennials that are relatively easy (especially when you compare them to fussy plants such as delphinium!), but they do require some attention (such as deadheading and dividing).

Finally, three trowels go to moderately easy perennials. These are plants that require average, routine maintenance, whether that means deadheading, pinching to promote a nice bushy shape, or simply monitoring the plant to be sure it stays healthy.

GOOD GARDEN PRACTICE

It's good garden practice to examine plants as often as possible so that you know what is going on from day to day. If you can't get to your plants daily, try reserving at least one day a week for a garden checkup. Look closely at each plant for signs of potential problems, such as yellowing leaves, insect tracks, and munched leaves.

Finding the Plants

The perennials are listed here by their Latin names, with the common names below. Remember, a plant's common name may vary from one part of the country to another and may also apply to more than one plant. If you order "daisies" you might not get the particular plants you want. It's best to try to learn the Latin names of plants so that you be sure you get the right ones.

Plant Portraits

Achillea

Yarrow
Zones: 3–10
Height: *A. filipendulina*, 3$^1/_2$–4 feet; hybrids, 3 feet
Sun: Full sun

Achillea filipendulina
'Gold Plate'

What: Yarrow's yellow, flat-topped flower clusters above ferny, gray-green foliage appear throughout the summer and make great cut flowers and pretty dried flowers for winter bouquets. Fernleaf yarrow (*A. filipendulina*) is the tallest of the yarrows and grows to about 4 feet. The cultivar 'Gold Plate' grows to 5 feet and has very showy bright gold flowers. *A.* 'Moonshine' has primrose yellow flowers; *A.* 'Coronation Gold' has bright mustard yellow flowers.

Where: Depending on its size, yarrow is perfect in the front, middle, or back of a border with other warm colors. The softer yellow *A.* 'Moonshine' is very pretty alongside meadow sage (*Salvia* × *superba*). Plant it with other perennials that attract butterflies, such as butterfly weed (*Asclepias tuberosa*), catmint (*Nepeta* × *mussinii*), baby's breath (*Gypsophila paniculata*), and bee balm (*Monarda didyma*).

How: Plant yarrow in a sandy soil with good drainage and full sun. *Achillea* is easy and tolerates humidity, poor soils, alkaline soils, and even drought conditions. Cut plants back to ground level in the fall to neaten up the garden. Plants should be divided every couple of years to keep the stock vigorous. Low maintenance.

Trowels: 🌱

Aconitum carmichaelii

Azure monkshood
Zones: 2–9
Height: 4 feet
Sun: Full sun or partial shade

What: Monkshood is a very pretty plant with rich, glossy green foliage and hooded dark blue flowers (that resemble the cowled hoods of monks) along the tall stems. It's one of the last plants to flower in the season and gives great blue color to the fall garden. However, it's important to note that all parts of the plant are poisonous. Although this is no reason not to grow monkshood, it may be unwise to use it if you have young children or pets who may get near it.

Aconitum carmichaelii

Where: Use monkshood as a substitute for more finicky delphiniums, which are also tall, blue, and stately. It looks great toward the back of the border with white plants such as bugbane (*Cimicifuga racemosa*).

How: Monkshood is not difficult to grow—give it a soil enriched with compost or well-rotted manure and a mulch in summer to help retain moisture. You may need to water in dry spells and plants may need staking. Divide plants in the spring or fall every three years to increase stock. Wear protective gloves when working with monkshood to avoid contact with the poisonous sap.

Trowels: 🌱 🌱 🌱

Agapanthus africanus

Blue African lily, agapanthus
Zones: 9–10
Height: $1\frac{1}{2}$–2 feet
Sun: Full sun

Agapanthus africanus

What: Agapanthus has elegant, large umbels of blue or white flowers on strong stalks that appear well above the glossy, straplike foliage throughout summer. Agapanthus is an attractive plant even when not flowering. These are wonderful plants in frost-free areas, where they can be enjoyed year-round outdoors; in cooler regions they can be grown in containers and wintered-over indoors. *Agapanthus* 'Headbourne' hybrids have very pretty creamy white or blue flowers and are slightly hardier than *A. africanus*, to zone 8.

Where: Agapanthus is perfect for containers in full sun. Where the plants are hardy, place them in large clumps in long borders. Agapanthus tolerates seashore conditions well.

How: Give agapanthus full sun and a well-drained, fertile soil. Plants in containers will flower best if they are root bound and placed in a coarse, sandy soil. Give plants a liquid fertilizer (10–10–10) at the start of the season, and water throughout as needed. Plants will increase slowly, and in a few years you can divide the roots for more stock. Remove the plant from its container (you may need to cut the container to pry the roots out) and use a sharp knife to divide the heavy crown. Replant new divisions in containers that fit the new plants snugly. Its best to divide in the spring, and avoid planting too deeply. Agapanthus needs regular deadheading but not staking. Winter care for agapanthus depends on the zone you are in: Where plants are not hardy, bring the containers indoors before the first frost, place them in a sunny spot, and keep the plants slightly moist throughout the winter. Where plants are hardy, leave them outdoors. Give them a 2- to 3-inch winter mulch such as compost.

Trowels: 🌱 🌱

Alchemilla mollis

Lady's-mantle
Zones: 3–9
Height: 1–2 feet
Sun: Full sun or partial shade

Alchemilla mollis

What: Lady's-mantle has tiny chartreuse flowers in frothy sprays in early summer, downy, rounded leaves, and a floppy habit that make it a good ground cover. The flowers are similar to baby's breath and bloom for a long time. Use them for fresh or dried arrangements instead of baby's breath for an interesting and different effect.

Where: Lady's-mantle works well in the front of the border—let it spill over the garden bed. The pretty, grayish green foliage combines well with white, yellow, blue, and purple flowers. Try it next to blue-flowering speedwell (*Veronica incana*).

How: Lady's-mantle grows in full sun or partial shade, provided the soil is well draining and moisture retentive. Plants in full sun will need a summer mulch to keep the soil cool. Water during very hot spells. The foliage may burn in full sun, turning brown; if this happens cut it back to the ground. There is no need to deadhead. Divide in early spring before it starts blooming or in the fall. Low maintenance.

Trowels: 🌱 🌱

How: Give columbine a well-drained, fertile soil; the plants may rot in a soil that is not well drained. Columbine needs to be kept moist, so provide water as necessary during hot weather. In the South, plants will need a little shade. Spider mites can be a problem in hot areas, but you can control them by cutting back the foliage after the plants flower. These are short-lived perennials; but if you let them go to seed (don't deadhead), you'll get seedlings everywhere the following spring. The seedlings will not bloom in the same color as their parents, but they may be pretty just the same. If you want to transplant the seedlings, dig up the small plant, trying to get all the roots. It's best to transplant when the seedlings are still small, as older plants resent being moved.

Trowels: ✔ ✔

Artemisia

Wormwood, artemisia
Zones: 5–10
Height: *A. schmidtiana*, 6–8 inches; *A. ludoviciana*, 2–3½ feet
Sun: Full sun

Artemisia ludoviciana 'Silver King'

What: Artemisias are wonderful foliage plants with aromatic leaves. The silvery gray, filigreed foliage of *A. ludoviciana* grows about 3 feet high and spreads as wide. Some artemisias, such as *A. schmidtiana*, are hardier, to zone 4. *A. schmidtiana* 'Silver Mound' stays compact, growing to 1 foot. Plants spread rapidly to form a patch.

Where: Silver-toned artemisias enhance bright colors and add a soft touch to a blue-gray-lavender (cool) color scheme. The smaller forms can be used in the front of the border, and the taller forms in the middle. Use artemisias with Frikart's aster (*Aster × frikartii*), because they both have a silvery tint.

How: Give artemisia a sunny position and an average or even poor or dry soil. To increase stock and keep the plants looking neat, dig and divide them every spring and replant them 1 foot apart, increasing your patch of artemisia. Trim the plants back in the spring when you see new growth.

Trowels: 🌱 🌱

Aruncus dioicus

Goatsbeard
Zones: 3–9
Height: 4–7 feet
Sun: Full sun or partial shade

Aruncus dioicus

What: Goatsbeard is a tall plant with giant, feathery plumes of creamy white flowers on sturdy stems in summer. Flowers last up to four weeks. Plants are shrublike with many stems and are virtually trouble free.

Where: Use goatsbeard as a specimen plant in the back of the border and in the shade garden. It's height gives it a dramatic presence, and the white flowers brighten up a shady nook.

How: Give goatsbeard a rich, moist soil and provide water throughout the growing season as necessary. They will live quite happily undisturbed—no staking, no deadheading, no cutting back. They aren't even bothered much by pests or diseases. Low maintenance.

Trowels: 🌱

Asclepias tuberosa

Butterfly weed
Zones: 3–10
Height: 1–2$^1/_2$ feet
Sun: Full sun

Asclepias tuberosa

What: Butterfly weed is a vigorous grower (that's why it's called "weed") with masses of brilliant orange, red, or yellow flower clusters that bloom in summer. It can beat out the most tenacious weeds and win a place in any garden. Butterflies love this plant and are all over it in the early summer.

Where: Butterfly weed will spread to several times its height and is beautiful naturalized in a meadow garden. It also grows well in large containers. Or use it toward the middle of a border with other hot colors.

How: Butterfly weed thrives in dry and poor soil and puts up with just about everything except a soggy soil. These plants are some of the last to come up in the spring, so be careful not to injure the crowns—they will be hard to see.

Trowels: 🌱

Aster × frikartii

Frikart's aster
Zones: 5–10
Height: 2–3 feet
Sun: Full sun or partial shade

What: Frikart's aster is an excellent plant for its fragrant, lavender blue, daisy-shaped flowers, which appear late in the summer and last practically year-round where winters are mild. *A. ×* *frikartii* 'Monch' is a popular cultivar with a multitude of hyacinth blue flowers tinged with silver. Plants attract butterflies and make good cut flowers.

Aster × frikartii 'Monch'

Where: Use Frikart's aster in the front of the border, letting it spill over. The blue color is beautiful with mums in a border designed for fall color.

How: Most asters thrive in a well-enriched, fertile soil and full or partial sun. Not enough water and poor air circulation can create the disease powdery mildew. To avoid this, water deeply during dry spells, and give the plants plenty of air circulation. Cut back the plants after flowering in the fall, and divide them every two years in the spring. Plants in zone 5 may need an evergreen bough winter mulch for protection.

Trowels: ✍ ✍

Astilbe × arendsii

False spirea, astilbe
Zones: 4–8
Height: $1^1/_2$–4 feet
Sun: Full sun or partial shade

What: Astilbe's flowers form in panicles of white and cream as well as many shades of pink and red above ferny foliage. Some plants will flower early in the summer, some late. One of the prettiest red-flowering hybrids is *A. × arendsii* 'Fanal', which grows to 2 feet and flowers early in summer. 'Rheinland' is a gorgeous, deep rose color that also flowers early. The foliage stays attractive all season.

Where: Use astilbes in the shade garden with Solomon's seal (*Polygonatum odoratum*), hostas, and ferns. The taller forms make dramatic accent plants in any garden as well as in large containers.

How: Plant astilbes in full sun or partial shade with lots of organic matter. Give plants a mulch to keep them cool in summer, and provide plenty of water. No need to deadhead or stake. Divide plants every three or four years to increase stock and keep plants growing vigorously. You'll need to use a sharp knife to cut through the heavy, fleshy roots.

Trowels: ✧

Astilbe × arendsii 'Rheinland'

Aurinia saxatilis

Basket-of-gold, goldentuft
Zones: 4–10
Height: 1–2 feet
Sun: Full sun

What: Basket-of-gold's abundance of bright yellow flower clusters appear in early spring. It forms a cushion of flowers that will cascade over walls. The gray-green leaves are also pretty.

Where: Use basket-of-gold for edging borders and beds, in the cracks of stone walls, and between paving units. Pair them with blue forget-me-nots (*Myosotis scorpioides*).

Aurinia saxatilis

How: Give basket-of-gold a sunny place in a dryish, well-drained garden. Shear the plants after they flower to maintain compact growth. These plants tolerate drought and demand little or no fertilizer.

Trowels: 🌱

Baptisia australis

Blue false indigo
Zones: 3–10
Height: 3–6 feet
Sun: Full sun or partial shade

What: Blue false indigo has rich, blue flowers on tall, stately spikes that appear in early summer and clover-shaped green leaves. This plant is native to the southern United States.

Baptisia australis

Where: Use blue false indigo in the middle of a border with peonies and irises, which bloom at the same time. You can also use it as a hedge, shearing it to create a compact shape.

How: Blue false indigo does well in full sun or shade and in an average soil. Because it develops long taproots, it doesn't like being moved unless you can successfully dig out the entire root. Remove faded flowers to prolong flowering, which also prevents the plant from forming seedpods. Or let them go to seed if you want the plants to self-sow, which they will easily.

Trowels: 🌱 🌱 🌱

Boltonia asteroides

Boltonia
Zones: 3–10
Height: 4–7 feet
Sun: Full sun or partial shade

Boltonia asteroides
'Snowbank'

What: Boltonia is a large perennial with many branches and a multitude of daisylike flowers in pink or white with yellow centers. It flowers in late summer and fall and resembles baby's breath (*Gypsophila paniculata*) but grows much bigger. 'Snowbank' has beautiful white flowers and grows to just 4 feet.

Where: Mass boltonia in the back of borders or combine it with purple coneflower, rudbeckia, and other native American plants for a natural look in the garden.

How: Boltonia is easy and undemanding. It tolerates heat, humidity, and most soils. Taller plants may need staking, but compact 'Snowbank' does not. Divide the plants every two to three years.

Trowels: 🔱 🔱

Brunnera macrophylla

Siberian bugloss
Zones: 3–10
Height: 1$^1/_2$–2 feet
Sun: Full sun or partial shade

What: Siberian bugloss has very pretty, heart-shaped leaves that form in neat clumps with sprays of tiny blue flowers in the spring, about the same time you see daffodils and forsythia in bloom. The leaves last until frost.

Where: Use bugloss as a ground cover under deciduous trees, under shrubs, in the shade garden as edging plants, or toward the front of any border.

How: Siberian bugloss prefers shade and a moist, fertile soil but tolerates dry shade. They bloom as well in sun as they do in shade. These plants are low maintenance, with the exception of some slug monitoring that you may have to do. They will self-sow.

Brunnera macrophylla

Trowels: 🌱 🌱

Campanula

Bellflower
Zones: 3–10
Height: *C. carpatica*, 8–15 inches; *C. lactiflora*, $3^1/_2$–5 feet; *C. persicifola*, 2–3 feet
Sun: Full sun or partial shade

What: The *Campanula* genus is large and includes lots of perennials and biennials, many of which are great for beds and borders. Peach-leaf bellflower (*C. persicifolia*) is an erect plant with purplish blue or white bell-shaped flowers that appear in summer. Milky bellflower (*C. lactiflora*) is one of the tallest bellflowers, with large panicles of blue or white flowers. Carpathian bellflowers (*C. carpatica*) are low-growing

Campanula lactiflora

mounds of foliage with flowering stems about a foot high. These plants are evergreen in mild regions.

Where: Bellflowers are great for the middle or rear of a perennial border. The white-flowering campanulas look pretty in partial shade.

How: Give bellflowers a well-drained, fertile soil. They're easy to please, but slugs can be a nuisance. Divide the plants every three or four years in the spring for more stock. In hot climates, they may need some shade. Deadhead to get more blooms. Milky bellflower may need some staking. Plants spread freely by seed.

Trowels: 🌱 🌱

Canna × generalis

Canna hybrids
Zones: 8–10
Height: $1^1/_2$–9 feet
Sun: Full sun

What: Big and bold canna, with its huge, banana-like leaves and brilliantly colored flowers, is once again enjoying popularity, after having been relegated to the "too garish" pile for many years. Flowers appear in summer in clear orange, scarlet, yellow, white, or soft creamy pink; leaves are often reddish or even a variegated yellow and green. The 'Seven Dwarfs' strain is smaller than most cannas (3–5 feet) and offers a mix of colors. 'The President' is bright red and grows 6–9 feet tall.

Canna × generalis
'The President'

Where: A striking accent plant, tropical-looking canna is perfect in containers around pools and patios or planted (carefully, as it does make quite a statement) in a large mixed border.

How: Give canna a fertile soil enriched with compost. Water as necessary, with deep, long soaks, but don't let the soil remain too wet for long periods of time. Gardeners in the South can enjoy cannas year-round: Prune the old canna flower stems all the way down to the crowns after flowering; the plants will then send up new side shoots and successive flower stalks. Where plants are not hardy, cut them back to about 6 inches just after the first frost and store plants indoors in a cool, dry place. Plants can be set out in the spring, after the soil has warmed up. Dig and divide cannas in the fall or early spring when there is no active top growth. Monitor carefully for slugs and snails early in the spring: These pests often bite the foliage when it is still rolled up.

Trowels: 🥄 🥄 🥄

Cerastium tomentosum

Snow-in-summer
Zones: 3–10
Height: 6–12 inches
Sun: Full sun

What: Snow-in-summer is a wonderful ground cover, with silvery white foliage and pure white, star-shaped flowers in late spring and early summer. Plants form mats that spread quickly.

Where: Use snow-in-summer in rock gardens and in any garden where water is a premium. These plants will even grow in pure sand. This is an effective and very pretty ground cover for banks.

Cerastium tomentosum

How: Give snow-in-summer a well-draining, sandy soil in a sunny location. Cut back after flowering to neaten up the plants. They require no watering and no fertilizing. Very low maintenance.

Trowels: 🥄

Ceratostigma plumbaginoides

Plumbago, leadwort
Zones: 5–10
Height: 6–12 inches
Sun: Full sun or partial shade

What: Plumbago is a low, spreading plant with bright blue flowers in clusters that appear in late summer and early fall. In the fall, the leaves are tinged with red.

Ceratostigma plumbaginoides

Where: Use plumbago in the front of the border, as an edging along walkways, and in containers.

How: Give plumbago a well-drained soil and plenty of organic matter. Water if needed throughout the growing season. In colder areas, the plants will die back naturally and need a winter mulch, such as pine boughs. In warmer areas, these woody plants won't die back, so they will need to be cut back hard, almost to the ground. These are drought- and seashore-tolerant plants.

Trowels: 🌱 🌱

Cimicifuga racemosa

Bugbane, black snakeroot
Zones: 3–10
Height: 3–8 feet
Sun: Full sun or partial shade

What: Bugbane is native to the northeastern United States and is a tall, dramatic plant with spires of pure white flowers on wiry stems in summer. The flowers, which resemble candelabras or long wands, are wonderfully fragrant.

Where: A great plant for the back of the border or woodland garden, bugbane is a slender plant with nice height that fits well among other tall perennials or shrubs.

How: Give bugbane a well-drained soil enriched with humus, and plant it in a cool moist place. The plants need a little shade in hotter climates. No staking or deadheading is required. Bugbane can remain untouched for years without being divided. Low maintenance.

Trowels: 🖊

Cimicifuga racemosa

Convallaria majalis

Lily-of-the-valley
Zones: 3–9
Height: 8 inches
Sun: Partial shade, shade

What: Lily-of-the-valley's waxy, white, bell-shaped flowers grow on 6-inch stems and are wonderfully fragrant. They appear in late spring with the plant's large, oval-shaped leaves. Lily-of-the-valley makes an excellent ground cover.

Where: Plant this old-fashioned favorite wherever you can. Ideally you want lily-of-the-valley where you will enjoy it—by entryways, along paths, or massed in shade as part of your foundation planting. You can bring the delicious scent inside by filling small vases with the cut flowers.

Convallaria majalis

How: Lily-of-the-valley plants begin as pips, which are roots that you plant horizontally in a shallow hole in the soil. Give the plants a rich, well-drained soil with plenty of moisture. These plants are basically trouble free, requiring only a dressing of humus or composted manure each spring to enrich the soil. If the foliage begins to dry out in the late summer or look shabby, simply cut the plants back to the ground. You can divide established clumps of lily-of-the-valley in the early spring for additional plants.

Trowels: 🌱 🌱

Coreopsis verticillata

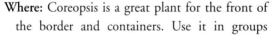

Threadleaf coreopsis
Zones: 3–10
Height: 18 inches
Sun: Full sun

What: Coreopsis has pretty, daisylike yellow flowers with slightly darker centers and light green, ferny foliage. Plants bloom faithfully all summer. 'Moonbeam' is a nice primrose yellow color.

Coreopsis verticillata

Where: Coreopsis is a great plant for the front of the border and containers. Use it in groups of five for the best effect. Or plant it on sunny slopes and in wildflower meadows.

How: Coreopsis is easy: It's drought and heat tolerant and needs only sun and an average soil. If you deadhead early in the season after first flowering, you'll get a second flush of flowers in the fall. Plants are easy to dig and divide in the spring or fall. In the fall, cut them back to the ground.

Trowels: 🌱

Crambe cordifolia

Colewort, giant kale
Zones: 6–9
Height: 4–7 feet
Sun: Full sun

Crambe cordifolia

What: Colewort is a stout, bushy plant with tiny white flowers in late spring and early summer that cover the plant. Flowers are starry and scented, resembling baby's breath (*Gypsophila paniculata*) in their airy habit, but these plants are much larger, and the base of colewort is a mound of large, dark cabbage-like leaves.

Where: Colewort is best in large gardens. It's size makes it ideal for the back of the border.

How: Give colewort a deep, well-drained soil, because the plants develop long roots. Water deeply when necessary throughout the growing season. Plants may need staking. In the fall, cut plants back to neaten up their appearance. Colewort doesn't need to be divided and is likely to grow happily with little maintenance.

Trowels: 🔧 🔧

Dendranthema × grandiflorum

Garden mum
Zones: 4–10
Height: 1–3 feet
Sun: Full sun

What: These plants used to be called *Chrysanthemum × morifolium* and are the popular mums you see everywhere in flower in the fall. There are many colors—everything but blue.

Where: Mums are wonderful in large containers, in the front of beds or borders, or edging walkways. Use them in a fall-flowering border with ornamental grasses, asters (*Aster × frikartii*), and boltonia (*Boltonia asteroides*).

How: Many gardeners buy garden mums in the fall and use them as annuals, discarding them after they flower. It's better (and less expensive) to plant young mums in the spring. Pinch them back as they are growing—until about July 1 where the growing season is short and until the end of July in warmer climates—to get full, bushy plants. The plants should be divided every other fall for more stock and to keep them healthy. In the fall, trim them back to the ground.

Dendranthema × grandiflorum 'Cornhusker'

Trowels: 🌱 🌱

Dianthus plumarius

Cottage pink, dianthus
Zones: 4–10
Height: 6–12 inches
Sun: Full sun

What: Dianthus's white, red, or pink flowers have the spicy fragrance of carnations and bloom from summer to fall. The foliage is either gray-green or blue-green and evergreen where winters are mild.

Dianthus plumarius

Where: Let dianthus tumble and flop onto paths; use it in the rock garden, cottage garden, edging a path, or in the front of any border.

How: Give dianthus a well-drained, gritty soil. Deadhead after they flower, and they will bloom again. Water as often as often as necessary, but don't let them live in a soggy soil. These plants are fine in humidity. Provide a winter mulch of evergreen boughs in zones 4 and 5. Dianthus are long-blooming when deadheaded regularly. In the fall, cut back the stems to a few inches above the ground.

Trowels: 🌱 🌱

Dicentra

Bleeding-heart

Zones: 3–10

Height: *D. eximia*, 10–12 inches; *D. spectabilis*, 2$^1/_2$ feet

Sun: Partial shade, shade

Dicentra spectabilis 'Alba'

What: Bleeding-hearts are well-loved plants for their pink or white flowers, which appear in spring, dangling from arching stems. *D. spectabilis* is a wonderful plant with a loose habit; fringed bleeding-heart (*D. eximia*) will flower intermittently all summer. The foliage is ferny and fine.

Where: Use bleeding-hearts in the cottage garden, the foreground of borders, and in wildflower gardens. They look nice combined with other shade-tolerant plants, such as astilbes and hostas.

How: Bleeding-hearts are not demanding: They need only a well-drained soil enriched with humus and a soil that is neither too wet nor too dry. Water as often as needed. These plants can begin to look straggly when the foliage dies after blooming, but resist cutting back as they need the foliage to pho-tosynthesize. Let it turn completely brown before cutting back. To keep fringed bleeding-heart (*D. eximia*) blooming, remove faded flowers regularly. Plants self-sow, and seedlings will emerge everywhere. Give the plants plenty of shade in hot areas.

Trowels: 🌱 🌱

Digitalis

Foxglove
Zones: 4–9
Height: $1^1/_2$–3 feet
Sun: Full sun or partial shade

Digitalis purpurea 'Foxy'

What: The many species of foxglove are garden favorites for perennial borders and have long spikes of white, pink, purple, or yellow tubular-shaped flowers in late spring and early summer. Common foxglove (*D. purpurea*) is a biennial that sows itself freely. All species make wonderful cut flowers.

Where: Use foxglove in classic English cottage garden borders. The soft colors mix well with just about all other colors, and the shape of the plants add a strong vertical accent to the garden. They are also charming in an informal setting, such as a woodland garden.

How: Give foxgloves a soil enriched with organic matter. The plants will need some shade in hot areas where they may also be evergreen. Cut them back after flowering for a second flush of flowers. Be on the lookout for snails and slugs. Plants self-sow readily. In the fall, cut the flower stems back to just above the ground; in cooler climates, provide a winter mulch after the ground freezes. Watch for volunteer seedlings in the spring.

Trowels: 🌱 🌱

Echinacea purpurea

Purple coneflower
Zones: 3–10
Height: 2–4 feet
Sun: Full sun or partial shade

Echinacea purpurea

What: Coneflower, a native wildflower, has enormous, daisy-shaped, magenta-rose flowers with big, showy disks in the center. The best-known cultivar is surely *E. purpurea* 'Magnus', which has big 6-inch-wide flowers in July and August. Coneflower has coarse foliage and grows to about 4 feet. White forms are also available.

Where: Coneflower is very pretty anywhere: in the cut garden, in a meadow, in any garden scheme with hot or cold colors. Use it toward the back of the border.

How: Plants need average soil and full or partial sun. Before plants flower, pinch to get a nice shape. The foliage can begin to look raggedy toward the end of the season; cut back plants to the ground in the fall. Coneflower can withstand drought and seashore conditions. Low maintenance.

Trowels: 🌱

Echinops ritro

Globe thistle
Zones: 3–10
Height: 2–3 feet
Sun: Full sun

What: Silvery blue flower globes appear from summer to early fall on these plants. The foliage is coarse, thistle-like, and prickly. 'Veitch's Blue' grows to 3 feet and has metallic blue flower heads and gray-green foliage. They make wonderful fresh and dried flowers.

Where: Globe thistle is a great accent plant with its silvery blue balls above the foliage. Use it toward the back of a border with other cool-colored, tall plants, such as monkshood (*Aconitum carmichaelii*).

How: These plants require very little beyond a sunny location and average soil. Deadhead for continuous bloom. The plants will self-sow.

Trowels: 🪏

Echinops ritro

Gaillardia × *grandiflora*

Blanketflower
Zones: 3–10
Height: 2–3 feet
Sun: Full sun

What: Blanketflower is a native plant and can be found growing wild in many parts of the United States. The large, daisy-like flowers with bright bands of colors—red, orange, and yellow—in summer to fall make excellent cut flowers.

Gaillardia × *grandiflora*

Where: Use blanketflower in the cutting garden or let it naturalize in a meadow. These plants also do well in containers. They can tolerate seashore conditions.

How: Give blanketflower a free-draining, dryish soil. These plants are short-lived but heat and drought tolerant, and there's no need to deadhead. Low maintenance.

Trowels: ✐

Geranium

Cranesbill, hardy geranium
Zones: 5–10
Height: 1–2 feet
Sun: Full sun or partial shade

What: Cranesbill is not the plant commonly called "geranium" (which is really, botanically speaking, a member of the genus *Pelargonium*). In fact, cranesbill doesn't look anything like that geranium. These plants are low-growing mounds of green foliage with pink, rose, magenta, blue, or lilac flowers. One of the most popular cranesbills is *G.* 'Johnson's Blue' with a sprawling habit and violet-blue flowers. *G. endressii* 'Wargrave Pink' is a light rosy color. They flower in spring to late spring. With deadheading you'll get a second flush of flowers.

Geranium
'Johnson's Blue'

Where: Cranesbill plants are perfect in the front of a border—they all look good next to catmint (*Nepeta* × *mussinii*)—and in a garden of peonies and irises.

How: For all their garden beauty, cranesbills are not fussy plants. They need average soil and full sun or partial shade; they'll rebloom with deadheading. Divide the plants in the fall. If they sprawl too much after flowering, cut back to new foliage.

Trowels: ✐ ✐

Gypsophila paniculata

Baby's breath
Zones: 3–10
Height: $1\frac{1}{2}$–4 feet
Sun: Full sun

Gypsophila paniculata
'Early Snowball'

What: Tiny, star-shaped, white or pink flowers cover this plant in summer, making it appear billowy and light. The foliage is a soft gray-green. Baby's breath makes excellent fresh-cut flowers (all florists know this) as well as dried flowers. *G. paniculata* 'Bristol Fairy' is probably the best known cultivar, with double white flowers on 3-foot stems. *G. paniculata* 'Gypsy' grows about 1 foot tall and carries sweet pompom-like flowers.

Where: Use baby's breath in any garden plan toward the middle of the border, wherever a light, airy touch is needed. Perfect in the cutting garden.

How: Give baby's breath full sun and a well-drained soil. Plants may need support, which you can provide by tying string around them to keep them up or by planting them next to plants that they can lean against for support. Baby's breath should not be transplanted, because it develops a long taproot. In the fall, cut off the old flower stems.

Trowels: 🌱 🌱 🌱

Helenium autumnale

Sneezeweed
Zones: 3–10
Height: 4–5 feet
Sun: Full sun

Helenium autumnale
'Moorheim Beauty'

What: Sneezeweed is a tall plant with beautiful daisylike orange or yellow flowers with chestnut rays that bloom in late summer and early fall. 'Butterpat' is very long blooming, with all yellow flowers. Great cut flowers.

Where: Use sneezeweed anywhere you want bright fall color. It's perfect for the cutting garden or in a butterfly garden with other plants that attract butterflies. Use it in the back of an informal border with other hot colors such as bee balm (*Monarda didyma*) and black-eyed Susans (*Rudbeckia fulgida*).

How: Sneezeweed is easy in any average soil and grows well in damp soils. Water deeply throughout the growing season. Deadhead for more bloom. Divide every three years in spring or fall. Tall cultivars may need staking.

Trowels: 🌱 🌱

Heliopsis helianthoides

False sunflower
Zones: 4–9
Height: 5 feet
Sun: Full sun

What: False sunflower is related to the common annual sunflower but has a slightly more refined appearance with smaller flower heads. The bright yellow or deep orange flowers appear in summer and early fall on tall stalks. Their long stems make them great cut flowers.

Where: Use false sunflower in informal settings or in the back of the border with other hot colors.

How: Give false sunflower a well-drained soil enriched with organic matter and water throughout the season. However, the plants will tolerate drought and poor soils. Deadhead for more flowers. No staking is necessary. The plants are relatively free of pests and disease. Low maintenance.

Heliopsis helianthoides 'Ballerina'

Trowels: ✐

Hemerocallis

Daylily hybrids
Zones: 3–10
Height: 1–4 feet
Sun: Full sun or partial shade

What: Easy! Daylilies are great, tough plants with classic, trumpet-shaped flowers in wonderful colors such as peach, pink, gold, orange, rose, cream, scarlet, yellow, and many, many others, everything but blue and white. Each individual flower blooms for just one day, but with many plants and different cultivars, you'll have daylilies flowering from spring to fall.

Hemerocallis 'Pompian Rose'

Where: One of the prettiest gardens is a daylily and daffodil border. Both plants have the same straplike foliage, and they provide continuous bloom from early spring when the daffodils come up to late summer with daylilies. Group orange-flowering daylilies next to purple-flowering plants such as globe thistle (*Echinops ritro*) and bright yellow daylilies with blue-flowering plants such as meadow sage (*Salvia × superba*). Use daylilies on a bank for erosion control.

How: Plant daylilies in an average soil and water regularly when plants are in bloom. Deadhead to keep plants looking neat. Give daylilies a light application of a balanced fertilizer at the beginning of the season. When daylily clumps have more than five or six fans (usually after three to five years), you can divide the plants for more stock. Wait until the weather cools in the fall, dig up the entire clump, and use your fingers or spading forks to pry the individual plants apart. Snap them into two or more pieces. Replant the same day. Pests and diseases are rarely a problem.

Trowels: ✓

Heuchera

Coralbells
Zones: 3–10
Height: 1–1^1/$_2$ feet
Sun: Full sun or partial shade

What: Coralbells are North American native plants that have tiny clouds of red, pink, or white flowers from spring to summer on wiry stems. Try *H.* 'Palace Purple', which has huge bronze-red leaves all year round and 18-inch sprays of small white flowers in August and September. These also make pretty cut flowers.

Where: Plant coralbells in the front of a border or in a woodland or shade garden with hostas and lily-of-the-valley (*Convallaria majalis*).

Heuchera × brizoides

How: Give coralbells full sun or partial shade in hotter areas. They need a soil that is well drained and enriched with organic matter. Water during dry spells. Divide every three to four years in the spring or when plants are producing fewer flowers. In the fall, cut the plants back to the ground.

Trowels: 🍃 🍃

Hosta

Plantain lily
Zones: 3–9
Height: 1–2 feet
Sun: Partial shade, shade

Hosta undulata

What: Hostas are easy and attractive foliage plants. New cultivars appear on the market every day, attesting to their huge popularity. While the foliage is the main attraction, white, lavender, or violet flowers appear above the foliage in summer. There are literally hundreds of cultivars available. *H. sieboldiana* has the largest leaves, in gray-green or bluish green. *H. fortunei* has broad foliage in a pretty sage green color. Wavy-leaf plantain (*H. undulata*) has wavy leaves with a broad cream stripe in the centers or on the edges.

Where: Hostas are great additions to the shade or woodland garden with heucheras, Solomon's seal (*Polygonatum odoratum*), and ferns. Mass them under deciduous trees or along a shaded wall. Choose a variety of hostas and plant along a shady path.

How: Give hostas a soil enriched with plenty of organic matter and light shade. Water throughout the growing season. Be on the lookout for slugs. The plants are easy to divide to increase stock, but are quite happy undivided.

Trowels: 🍃

Iris

Iris
Zones: 3–10
Height: 2–4 feet
Sun: Full sun or partial shade

Iris (bearded)
'Stepping Out'

What: There are many different species of irises, and although all share the traditional fleur-de-lis flower shape and sword-like foliage, they vary in size, width, and cultural needs. Descriptions of four of the most popular iris species follow.

Bearded iris is hardy in zones 3–10. Plants grow 1–3 feet high and should be planted in the fall. These plants are easy to grow, and they tolerate a wide range of conditions. Colors include pink, burgundy, orange, purple, lavender, white, yellow, light blue, and rose.

Japanese iris (*I. ensata*) is hardy to zones 5–10. Plants grow 2–3 feet high with blue, purple, pink, or white velvety-textured flowers. These are the last irises to bloom in the summer. Water during drought. Deadhead to keep the plants neat.

Siberian iris (*I. sibirica*) is hardy in zones 4–10. Plants grow 2–4 feet with delicate-looking white, blue, purple, red, or yellow flowers. 'Ruffled Velvet' has deep violet blooms with black-and-gold faces. The foliage turns a golden yellow in fall. These plants need a moist soil and full sun, and are the easiest of all irises. One trowel!

Yellow flag (*I. pseudacorus*) is hardy in zones 4–9. Plants grow 3–4 feet high with bright or creamy yellow flowers in June. They take full or partial sun and need a boggy soil.

Where: Mass bearded irises for best effect. Use Siberian irises in the border to bloom with peonies. Plant yellow flags by a pond or stream. Put Japanese irises in containers (with plenty of water) or in partial shade in a garden.

How: Irises grow by rhizomes, which are underground food-storage systems. Plant the rhizomes 1 or 2 inches below the surface in hot regions, but even more shallowly in cooler regions, with some of the rhizome showing on the surface. Water deeply during drought. Divide the plants every three to four years in late summer or early fall (except Siberian iris, which seldom needs dividing). Iris borers may bother these plants, causing infections; if so, destroy infected rhizomes to prevent the disease from spreading. Poor drainage and limited air circulation can result in a bacterial soft rot on the crowns. Remove diseased rhizomes, being careful not to injure the ones that are not sick. There's no need to cut back, and they require no mulching.

Trowels: 🌱 🌱 ; Siberian iris: 🌱

Lavandula angustifolia

English lavender
Zones: 3–9
Height: 2–3 feet
Sun: Full sun

What: Lavender has scented purple, white, or blue flowers in summer and attractive fragrant, silvery foliage all year. Technically, this plant is a sub-shrub because of its semiwoody base, which means that the plants won't die back in the winter. The cultivar 'Munstead' has lavender flowers and a nice compact form.

Where: Lavender is perfect for the front of a bed or border, for the cutting garden, for the herb garden, for containers, or for edging a pathway. Lavender looks wonderful massed for a formal look or used as an accent plant to soften edges around a garden bed.

Lavandula angustifolia
'Lady'

How: Give lavender an average to dry soil, not too rich. No need to cut plants back in the fall. Plants in zone 5 will need winter protection. After the ground freezes, place evergreen boughs loosely over the plants. Look for emerging leaves in early spring, then cut them back to tidy up the plants.

Trowels: ✐ ✐ ✐

Leucanthemum × superbum

Shasta daisy
Zones: 5–10
Height: 1–3 feet
Sun: Full sun or partial shade

What: Shasta daisy used to be called *Chrysanthemum × superbum,* and you may still find it with that name in some catalogs and nurseries. The white daisy flowers, blooming from early summer to fall, make great cut flowers.

Where: Use Shasta daisies in beds and borders for a wonderful cottage-like, informal look. Plant a stand of daisies by the back door. These plants are seashore tolerant and perfect by the beach.

Leucanthemum × superbum 'Becky'

How: Give Shasta daisies a rich, well-drained soil. Deadhead for repeat bloom. In the fall, cut back plants to the base to neaten up their appearance.

Trowels: ✐

Liatris spicata

Spike gayfeather, dense blazing star
Zones: 3–10
Height: 2–5 feet
Sun: Full sun

What: Spike gayfeathers are native American wildflowers that have white or purple flowers above tufts of grassy foliage and bloom from summer to fall. Flowers appear as bottle-brush spikes, opening from top to bottom (most flowers open from bottom to top). Gayfeather makes excellent fresh-cut or dried flowers and attracts butterflies.

Liatris spicata

Where: Use spike gayfeather in the middle of a border or in a meadow garden.

How: Plant spike gayfeather corms (underground storage stems) in a well-drained soil at a depth that's at least twice the width of the corms. These plants are drought resistant. There's no need to divide gayfeather; the plants self-sow, so look for seedlings in early spring. The seedlings can be dug and replanted (if you want to move them) the following spring. In the fall, cut the plants back to ground level.

Trowels: 🌱 🌱

Liriope muscari

Lilyturf
Zones: 5–10
Height: 1½–2 feet
Sun: Full sun or shade

Liriope muscari
'Variegata'

What: Lilyturf is an excellent low-growing ground cover with clusters of bright violet flowers in the fall and grasslike foliage. This tough plant can take more abuse than most ground covers.

Where: Plant lilyturf in the front of borders or under and around trees and tall shrubs.

How: Give lilyturf an average to dry soil. These plants tolerate a dry soil, even in shade, and colonize rapidly to form patches. Cut back the plants in spring to encourage new growth. You may have to work to control slugs and snails.

Trowels: 🌱 🌱

Lobelia

Cardinal flower, lobelia
Zones: 2–9
Height: *L. cardinalis*, 3–4 feet; *L. siphilitica*, 2–3 feet; *L. × speciosa*, 1½–5 feet
Sun: Full sun or shade

What: Cardinal flower has racemes of tall scarlet flowers above leafy clumps of foliage in late summer. Some of the most beautiful scarlet flowers are on

L. × *speciosa*, an extremely vigorous and hardy plant. Another great perennial lobelia is great blue lobelia (*L. siphilitica*), which grows about the same height but has spikes of deep blue flowers on bushy plants.

Where: Cardinal flowers are much-loved by hummingbirds: Plant them in a wildlife border or the middle of any flower border. Great blue lobelia is perfect naturalized beside a pond or stream or in the bog garden.

How: Lobelia prefers moist, rich soil and some shade. Give the plants a summer mulch to conserve moisture in the soil and a winter mulch of evergreen boughs to protect the plants in colder regions. Lobelia often self-sows.

Trowels: 🖉 🖉

Lobelia × *speciosa* 'Border Scarlet'

Lysimachia

Loosestrife
Zones: 3–10
Height: *L. nummularia*, 8 inches; *L. clethroides*, 2–3 feet
Sun: Full or partial sun

What: Gooseneck loosestrife (*L. clethroides*) is an upright plant with elegant clusters of pure white flowers in late summer to frost that arch—a group of them looks like a flock of geese. A very different plant in the *Lysimachia* genus is creeping Jenny (*L. nummularia* 'Aurea'), which is a

Lysimachia clethroides

low-growing, trailing plant with yellow foliage and gold flower clusters. Look for *L. nummularia* 'Golden Harvest' with foliage that is a warm and unusual chartreuse.

Where: Plants in the *Lysimachia* genus will run rampant through gardens with damp soil, so plant them where you want masses of them. They are wonderful naturalized beside ponds and banks.

How: Give lysimachia an average or damp soil and full or partial sun. Plants are easy to divide in the spring or fall for more stock. In the fall, cut back gooseneck loosestrife to ground level to neaten up its appearance.

Trowels: ✐

Malva

Mallow
Zones: 4–9
Height: 3–4 feet
Sun: Full sun

What: Mallow's white or pink bowl-shaped, hollyhock-like flowers appear from summer to frost, making this one of the longest blooming plants. Hollyhock mallow (*M. alcea*) has pink flowers along tall stems; musk mallow (*M. moschata*) is a bushier plant with pink or white flowers accented by dark green foliage.

Malva alcea 'Fastigiata'

Where: Mallow is perfect for the informal cottage garden. Plant it behind catmint (*Nepeta × mussinii*) and among other cottage garden plants, such as phlox (*Phlox paniculata*) and Shasta daisies (*Leucanthemum × superbum*).

How: Give mallow a well-drained sandy soil. They prefer a little shade where summers are hot. The plants are fast growing, short lived, and self sowing. Mallow is drought tolerant and low maintenance. Cut back the flowering stems to the ground for fall cleanup.

Trowels: ✐ ✐

Monarda didyma

Bee balm, Oswego tea
Zones: 4–10
Height: 2–3 feet
Sun: Full sun or partial shade

Monarda didyma
'Cambridge Scarlet'

What: Bee balm is a tall plant with aromatic dark green foliage and white, pink, red, or lavender flowers that appear on rounded heads throughout the summer. The plants are native to woods in the eastern United States. The flower heads remain attractive even after the plant has stopped flowering and make good cut flowers. Good choices for cultivars are 'Cambridge Scarlet', which has lacy scarlet flowers, and 'Marshall's Delight', with bright pink flowers.

Where: Bee balm is great for meadow gardens or for the middle or back of a border. It's a favorite among butterflies, hummingbirds, and bees.

How: Bee balm is easy to grow in a moisture-retentive soil enriched with organic matter. The plants need to be watered throughout the growing season as necessary. Cut them back hard in the fall, to ground level, and divide them every few years in spring to keep stock vigorous.

Trowels: ✐

Myosotis scorpioides

Forget-me-not

Zones: 3–8

Height: 6–10 inches

Sun: Full sun or partial shade

What: Forget-me-not's cornflower blue flowers grow in clusters from spring to early summer, and the oblong leaves form pretty mats of ground cover. Plants bloom for a long time.

Where: Grow forget-me-nots wherever it is wet: along streams and ponds and in bog gardens. These plants are great naturalized in a woodland garden.

Myosotis scorpioides

How: Plants thrive in cool, moist soils, spreading rapidly, forming many seeds, and self-sowing everywhere. It's not necessary to divide them; but if you want, do so in the spring or fall. Low maintenance.

Trowels: ✎

Nepeta × mussinii

Catmint

Zones: 3–10

Height: 1 foot

Sun: Full sun

What: Catmint's soft, lavender-blue flowers appear throughout summer, drifting above the small gray-green leaves. They have a floppy habit, and the flowers are fragrant and good for cutting.

Where: Use catmint in the front of a border or as an edging, letting it spill over onto paths. They're great by the seashore.

How: Plant catmint in full sun in a well-drained, dryish soil, and don't fertilize. Shear the plants after they flower for a second bloom. They are drought tolerant and won't need much water. Pest and diseases are rarely problems.

Trowels: ✓

Nepeta × mussinii 'Blue Wonder'

Nipponanthemum nipponicum

Nippon daisy, Montauk daisy
Zones: 5–10
Height: $1^1/_2$–$2^1/_2$ feet
Sun: Full sun

What: Nippon daisies used to be classified in the *Chrysanthemum* genus under the name *C. nipponicum*. These many-stemmed bushes with thick, glossy, dark green leaves have very big white flowers with green centers that bloom for many weeks in the fall. They perform best where growing seasons are long, such as the southeastern parts of the United States.

Nipponanthemum nipponicum

Where: Nippon daisies are great for seashores, where they hold up very well. Use one plant as an accent in the middle of the border.

How: Grow Nippon daisies in an average soil. Where summers are long, pinch the plants several times throughout the growing season to promote compact growth (the same way you would pinch mums). Don't pinch in cooler regions, because flowering will be delayed until after the frost. Instead, let the plants grow naturally. In the fall, cut them to ground level. No need to divide these plants, which are pest and disease free.

Trowels: 🌱 🌱 🌱

Oenothera

Sundrops
Zones: 4–10
Height: *O. missouriensis*, 9 inches; *O. tetragona*,
  2–3 feet
Sun: Full sun

Oenothera tetragona

What: Sundrops are low-growing, sprawling plants with fragrant 4-inch yellow or pink flowers in summer. Ozark sundrops (*O. missouriensis*) are tough, spreading wildflowers native to the Ozark Mountains. Sundrops (*O. tetragona*) have loose, leafy clumps of reddish stems, dark green leaves, and many bright yellow cup-shaped flowers throughout the summer. Seedpods follow, which are also attractive.

Where: Plant sundrops in the rock garden, Xeriscape garden, or anywhere water is a premium. They are great beside catmint (*Nepeta* × *mussinii*). These plants are also useful in gardens by the seashore.

How: Give sundrops an average soil. Although they are drought tolerant, water during dry weather, if it's possible. Give the plants a summer mulch to retain moisture and a winter mulch in cold regions. Deadhead to extend the blooming period, and divide the plants in spring to increase stock.

Trowels: 🌱

Paeonia lactiflora cultivars

Peony
Zones: 2–10
Height: 2–4 feet
Sun: Full sun

Paeonia lactiflora
'Jessie'

What: Peonies are richly textured, often fragrant, old-fashioned flowers that come in a wide variety of colors: shades of pink, yellow, cherry, and white. Some cultivars have single flowers, some have double (referring to the number of flower petals). Some cultivars bloom in early spring, while others bloom in late spring. This is one of the longest-lived perennials—it may live longer than you! Unfortunately, it's also one of the shortest flowering perennials, often flowering for only one week. The foliage continues looking good when plants stop flowering, turning a pretty bronze color in the fall. These are wonderful, fragrant, deer-resistant flowers. Try 'Amabillis' for its large, double, blush pink blooms or 'Bowl of Beauty' with its immense single flowers of delicate rose pink opening to soft yellow centers. Peonies make gorgeous cut flowers.

Where: Use peonies anywhere. They look great on their own in peony beds or combined in a perennial border with irises. The early-blooming species and cultivars are best in hot areas because they bloom before temperatures get too hot.

How: It's best to plant peonies in the fall when the plants are dormant. Give them a well-drained soil enriched with plenty of rotted manure or compost. Water deeply throughout the growing season. Plant the fleshy roots no deeper than $1/_2$ inch below the surface in the north. In the south, plant no deeper than 1 inch below the surface. Deep planting results in lack of flowers. For the biggest, most beautiful blooms, "disbud" flowers. This is a simple process: Pinch off the two flowers that appear on either side of the main flower to send the plant's energy to the single flower. Plants will need staking with a peony ring and deadheading after flowering. In the fall, cut the peonies to the ground after the foliage has turned yellow. No need to dig and divide. Add compost to the soil around plants every spring to enrich it.

Trowels: ✔ ✔ ✔

Papaver orientale

Oriental poppy
Zones: 3–9
Height: 2–4 feet
Sun: Full sun

Papaver orientale
'Prince of Orange'

What: The brilliant vermilion poppy flowers with the texture of crepe paper and black centers bloom in late spring and early summer and have always been popular in gardens. Cultivars are also available in pinks, oranges, and lavenders—try 'Pink Lassie' for a gentle light pink or 'Prince of Orange' for a fiery, tropical orange—but red poppies are still the ideal. Poppies make dazzling cut flower arrangements.

Where: The hot colors of poppies are flamboyant additions to sunny borders. Use any of them with baby's breath (*Gypsophila paniculata*) for a great combination of color and texture and to hide the coarse, hairy foliage that remains after flowering. The pink poppies look nice with gray foliage plants, such as artemisias.

How: Plant poppies in the fall when they are dormant. Poppy roots are long and brittle, so you must be careful not to damage them while planting. Give them a hole that is large enough to accommodate the roots in a well-drained soil enriched with organic matter. Staking is not necessary. These are hardy, long-lived plants that will need dividing only about every fifth year.

Trowels: ✔ ✔

Penstemon digitalis

Penstemon, beardtongue
Zones: 3–9
Height: 2–4 feet
Sun: Full

What: Native to the eastern and central United States, penstemon is a beautiful American wildflower with erect, showy white flowers that grow along the stems in late spring and early summer. *P. digitalis* 'Husker Red' has maroon foliage and white flowers.

Where: Use beardtongue in the middle of borders or naturalize them in a meadow garden with other American wildflowers.

Penstemon digitalis
'Husker's Red'

How: Give penstemon a well-drained, sandy soil in full sun. Don't mulch, don't fertilize. They can be temperamental, but not because they need attention: If conditions are right, they will grow well.

Trowels: ✓ ✓ ✓

Perovskia atriplicifolia

Russian sage
Zones: 5–10
Height: 3–5 feet
Sun: Full sun

What: Russian sage has graceful, lavender-blue flowers in middle to late summer on 3-inch stems of silvery gray foliage. The aromatic, square stems tell you this plant, like other sages, is actually in the mint family. Technically, Russian sage is a sub-shrub (as is lavender). The plants don't die back in the winter because the stems are woody.

Where: Russian sage is a perfect plant for an English cottage garden. Use it with peonies (*Paeonia lactiflora*), lavender (*Lavandula angustifolia*), and lamb's ears (*Stachys byzantina*) for a beautiful, soft, blue-gray border.

How: Russian sage likes a well-drained soil on the arid side. They like it hot and dry. It's best to leave the stems on plants throughout winter, cutting them back in spring to new growth. No need to deadhead or divide.

Trowels: 🥄 🥄

Perovskia atriplicifolia

Phlox paniculata

Border phlox
Zones: 3–9
Height: 2–5 feet
Sun: Full sun or partial shade

What: Phlox are fragrant, old-fashioned plants with flowers in white, pink, red, lavender, and purple (everything but blue and yellow) that bloom from summer to early fall. 'Bright Eyes' is the quintessential border plant with pink flowers and a crimson eye.

Where: Phlox are best planted in groups of at least three plants. Use them in the middle of the perennial bed or border.

Phlox paniculata
'Princess'

How: Give phlox a deep, porous, fertile soil enriched with a lot of organic material, because these are heavy feeders (they need a lot of fertilizing). Water deeply throughout the season, and provide them with a summer mulch to retain moisture. Phlox are prone to mildew, so avoid getting water on the foliage and thin new shoots as the plants are growing. Each plant should have no more than four to six strong stems, so cut off a few of the stems at the base to increase air circulation. Deadhead plants by pulling off each spent flower, and the plants will flower again. Not a low-maintenance plant but one of the best.

Trowels: ✓ ✓ ✓

Physostegia virginiana

Obedient plant
Zones: 3–10
Height: 3 feet
Sun: Full sun or partial shade

What: Obedient plants (called "obedient" because you can bend the flowers in any direction and they will stay there) are tall, long-flowering plants with snapdragon-like flowers in pale pink, purplish pink, or white from summer to fall. The plants attract butterflies.

Physostegia virginiana

Where: Obedient plants are invasive, so grow them where you want a wild garden look. The pale colors are especially pretty in shade.

How: Easy to grow, obedient plant thrives in moist soil and spreads rapidly. Plants need to be divided every two or three years.

Trowels: ✓ ✓

Platycodon grandiflorus

Balloon flower
Zones: 3–10
Height 1^1/$_2$–2^1/$_2$ feet
Sun: Full sun or partial shade

Platycodon grandiflorus 'Mariesii'

What: The buds of the balloon flower buds look like puffy balloons that open into white, pink, or blue cup-shaped flowers from summer to late summer. The foliage is a pretty gray-green color. The plants are long blooming and make good cut flowers.

Where: Use balloon flower in the middle of the border. The blue flowers are pretty with yellow daylilies or a bright yellow tickseed (*Coreopsis verticillata* 'Zagreb'). All the colors are pretty in light shade.

How: Balloon flower does well in average soil. The plants take time to get established, and foliage is slow to emerge in late spring so be careful not to injure it when weeding around them. No need to divide the plants, and they will self-sow.

Trowels: 🛠 🛠 🛠

Polygonatum odoratum

Solomon's seal
Zones: 5–9
Height: 1^1/$_2$–2 feet
Sun: Partial shade, shade

What: Solomon's seal's foliage is more significant than its flowers, though they too are very pretty. The long, strong stems arch, forming nearly horizontal branching. The tiny white flowers in late spring hang from the stems. In the fall, the foliage turns a pretty straw color. Variegated Solomon's seal shows up particularly well in the shade.

Where: Use Solomon's seal anywhere there is shade, such as in a woodland garden setting with astilbes, hostas, and ferns.

How: Give the plants a moist soil. They require little care beyond the right growing medium and shade. Solomon's seal roots shallowly, so be careful in early spring when the plants are just coming up.

Polygonatum odoratum 'Variegatum'

Trowels: 🌱 🌱

Primula

Primrose
Zones: 5–8
Height: *P. japonica* 1–2$^1/_2$ feet; *P. × polyantha*,
  10–15 inches
Sun: Partial shade

What: The *Primula* genus is one of the largest; in fact, there are so many species that are grouped into sections. While most primroses flower about the same time—in the spring and early summer—they vary widely in temperament and appearance. For instance, the Japanese primrose (*P. japonica*) in the Candelabra section has flowers

Primula × polyantha 'Dwarf Jewel' mix

high above the foliage in shades of white, pink, crimson, and reddish purple and is one of the very easiest to grow. A very different and fussier plant is the polyanthus primrose, also called English primrose (*P.* × *polyantha*), which comes in a wide variety of vibrant colors, all with a bright yellow eye.

Where: Use Japanese primroses in any soil that stays moist, such as along a pond or bog, or try them in large drifts with hostas and irises in a woodland garden. Polyanthus primroses are the perfect spring companion for tulips and other bulbs.

How: Give primroses a moisture-retentive soil. Add humus and organic matter to the soil to keep the area moist. Japanese primroses self-sow freely in wet places. Divide primroses every three or four years to keep the plants vigorous. They require no deadheading and no fall cleanup.

Trowels: 🌱 🌱 🌱

Rudbeckia fulgida

Black-eyed Susan, rudbeckia
Zones: 3–10
Height: 2–3 feet
Sun: Full sun or partial shade

What: Black-eyed Susans are garden favorites, with their daisy-like, sunny yellow, gold, or orange flowers that appear summer to fall. The best of the species is *R. fulgida* var. *sullivantii* 'Goldsturm' (and one of the longest names in Latin nomenclature). A name worth knowing, because these plants have a more compact shape and bigger flower than other rudbeckias.

Rudbeckia fulgida var. *sullivantii* 'Goldsturm'

Where: Mass rudbeckias with ornamental grasses and yarrow (*Achillea* spp.) to create a pretty meadow border. Use it in the middle of borders, in cutting gardens, and with other bright, bold colors that attract butterflies.

How: Give black-eyed Susans an average, well-drained soil. Deadhead to encourage more blooms. The plants are seashore, drought, and humidity tolerant. Not much bothers them. Cut them back to the ground for fall cleanup.

Trowels: 🖊

Salvia × superba

Meadow sage, salvia
Zones: 5–10
Height: $1^1/_2$–3 feet
Sun: Full sun

Salvia × superba

What: The *Salvia* genus is very large and includes tender perennials that are grown as annuals as well as true annuals. All salvias have square stems (since they are in the mint family) and aromatic foliage. *S. × superba* has spikes of violet-blue flowers in late spring through summer. 'East Friesland' is a good cultivar. (Don't confuse these ornamental plants with the culinary herb sage, *S. officinalis.*)

Where: Plant meadow sage along the front of a border. It looks pretty teamed up with yarrow (*Achillea filipendulina*) and other hot colors. Makes a great mass planting in any garden, including a butterfly garden.

How: Any well-drained soil is fine. Salvias love hot, dry sunny sites. The plants are best in a lean soil, so don't fertilize or add organic matter. Rich soil and fertilizer will cause the plants to flop over. Divide them only if the centers start to look thin. In the fall, cut the plants back to about 1 inch from the ground.

Trowels: 🖊 🖊

Scabiosa caucasica

Pincushion flower
Zones: 3–10
Height: $1^1/_2$–$2^1/_2$ feet
Sun: Full sun

What: The white, blue, or lavender blooms of the pincushion flower look a little like shaggy daisies and appear in mid to late summer. The 3-inch blossoms sit on long stalks and make pretty cut flowers.

Scabiosa caucasica
'Fama' and 'Alba'

Where: Mass pincushion flower for best effect. Use it in the middle of a border. Great for butterfly gardens.

How: Give pincushion flower a rich, well-drained soil. Water throughout the growing season as needed, and give the plants a little light shade in hot regions. Deadhead for more flowers, and divide in the spring or as needed to keep plants vigorous.

Trowels: 🌱 🌱

Sedum

Stonecrop, sedum
Zones: 4–10
Height: *S.* 'Autumn Joy', 2 feet; *S.* 'Ruby Glow', 8–10 inches;
  S. spectabile, $1^1/_2$–2 feet
Sun: Full sun or partial shade

What: Sedums are late-blooming succulent plants, flowering in mid to late summer. *S.* 'Autumn Joy' has domes of pink flowers that turn to a coppery color as the weather turns cold. The *Sedum* genus includes excellent, low-growing plants for use as ground cover and in rock gardens, such as *S.* 'Ruby Glow' with ruby red flowers and showy stonecrop (*S. spectabile*) with pink or red flowers.

Where: Use *S.* 'Autumn Joy' with ornamental grasses and purple coneflower (*Echinacea purpurea*). It is one of the last plants to flower in the late summer, and continues to look good if you leave the dried flower heads up all winter.

Sedum
'Autumn Joy'

How: Sedums require very little beyond full sun and an average soil. They can withstand heat and drought well. You can increase the number of plants by taking stem cuttings. Simply cut a piece of the stem, place it in water, and when the roots grow to about $^1/_4$ inch, transplant it to the garden.

Trowels: 🗡

Sempervivum tectorum

Hens and chickens
Zones: 5–10
Height: 1–1$^1/_2$ inches
Sun: Full sun

What: Hens and chickens are interesting plants that form mats of dense, stemless rosettes of succulent foliage with purple or reddish-pink centers.

Where: Use hens and chickens, which are a bit odd looking, for filling cracks and crevices in dry walls and rock gardens, between pavers, or as kind of a carpet around the edges of containers.

Sempervivum tectorum

How: Hens and chickens are easy to grow in poor soil. Even though they are succulents, they will need watering only when temperatures are very hot and dry.

Trowels: ✔

Sidalcea malviflora

Prairie mallow
Zones: 5–10
Height: 2–4 feet
Sun: Full sun or partial shade

What: Prairie mallow's branching spikes of small, silky flowers in shades of pink and magenta appear in summer. The flowers look like holly-hocks, and this plant is related to mallow (*Malva alcea*).

Where: Create a soft, cottage garden border with prairie mallow, hollyhocks (*Alcea rosea*), laven-der (*Lavandula angustifolia*), and lady's-mantle (*Alchemilla mollis*). Or naturalize them in a meadow garden.

Sidalcea malviflora

How: Prairie mallow are easy to grow in sun and a soil enriched with organic matter. Cut the plants back after flowering; they self-sow easily, but the colors are not always the best.

Trowels: ✔ ✔ ✔

Solidago hybrids

Goldenrod
Zones: 3–10
Height: $1^1/_2$–5 feet
Sun: Full sun or partial shade

Solidago
'Crown of Rays'

What: Goldenrod, a plant native to North America, can be seen in meadows and everywhere else in the summer months, growing wild with purple loosestrife. The hybrids' mustard yellow flowers appear in summer and early fall and are more attractive than their wildflower cousins. Goldenrod hybrids are great in gardens, and like the wild type, tend to be very aggressive growers. Try them in flower arrangements.

Where: Use tall goldenrod toward the back of borders and in cutting gardens. The plants attract butterflies and are wonderful with butterfly weed (*Asclepia tuberosa*) and bee balm (*Monarda didyma*).

How: Goldenrod needs a well-drained soil, and that's it. They are seashore and drought tolerant. The plants are very easy to grow and low maintenance. Cut them back in the fall to neaten up the garden.

Trowels: 🖌

Stachys byzantina

Lamb's ears
Zones: 4–10
Height: 1–1$^1/_2$ feet
Sun: Full sun or partial shade

What: The silvery foliage of lamb's ears is soft and velvety to the touch. These plants are mostly used for their foliage, although pretty magenta flowers grow along their stems in late spring and summer. The plants form a woolly mat of ground cover.

Where: Lamb's ears are a wonderful edging plant—let it sprawl and form a nice mat in the front of the border. It contrasts well with yellow-, pink-, and blue-flowering plants (*Achillea* 'Moonshine' is good choice).

Stachys byzantina

How: Give lamb's ears a fertile soil and moderate waterings. In the spring, run a rake lightly over the plants to remove old foliage leftover from the winter, and divide them as often as every year. Be careful not to water too much or they'll rot. The plants do best with no fertilizer.

Trowels: 🌱🌱

Stokesia laevis

Stoke's aster
Zones: 5–10
Height: 1–2 feet
Sun: Full sun or partial shade

What: The sky blue flowers of Stoke's asters are $2^{1}/_{2}$ inches wide and appear in summer and fall. White and pink cultivars are also available. The plants are long blooming and make great cut flowers.

Stokesia laevis

Where: Use Stoke's aster in the front of the border with other fall-flowering plants like *Sedum* 'Autumn Joy' and white-flowering boltonia.

How: Give Stoke's aster a well-draining, light, sandy soil. They like it on the dry side and are humidity and drought tolerant. Give them a light winter mulch in cold areas. The plants are evergreen in the South. In the fall, cut the plants back to neaten.

Trowels: ✒ ✒ ✒

Tanacetum parthenium

Feverfew
Zones: 4–10
Height: 1–3 feet
Sun: Full sun or partial shade

What: Feverfew used to be called *Chrysanthemum parthenium* but has recently been made part of the *Tanacetum* genus. It has tiny, daisy-like flowers from summer through early fall. This is a short-lived perennial that self-sows everywhere.

Where: Feverfew is very pretty in the front of beds and mixed borders and looks great next to annual larkspur (*Consolida ambigua*), which has blue flowers on tall spikes.

How: Give feverfew a light, sandy soil and water when necessary throughout the summer. In colder climates, the plants may need a winter mulch for protection. They can be divided for more stock in spring or fall; you'll also get more plants when they self-sow. Low maintenance.

Tanacetum parthenium

Trowels: ✎

Tradescantia virginiana

Spiderwort
Zones: 5–10
Height: 1–3 feet
Sun: Full sun or partial shade

What: Spiderwort is a quick-growing plant with lovely shades of blue, white, violet, pink, or magenta flowers in late spring to fall. The leaves are long and narrow. The plants flower for a long time. These plants grow by underground runners, forming dense clumps of foliage.

Where: Spiderwort is a wonderful plant when conditions are right, such as in woodland settings and shade gardens.

Tradescantia virginiana

How: Spiderwort is easy to grow in shade or partial shade and in any soil. It even performs well in poor soil with minimal watering and feeding. Cut plants back by half after they flower to get a second flush of flowers. The foliage can look untidy, so it's useful to plant spiderwort behind a smaller plant that can hide the foliage after spiderwort has stopped flowering. Cut back plants to ground level in the fall, and dig and divide in the spring for more stock.

Trowels: 🌱 🌱

Verbascum × hybridum

Mullein
Zones: 6–10
Height: 3–4 feet
Sun: Full sun

Verbascum
'Antique Shades'

What: Mulleins have soft, felt-like foliage and tall spires of pink, mauve, yellow, or white flowers. The plants are slender and statuesque. They make nice accents in the garden and in containers.

Where: The height and unusual shape of mullein makes it unique in any setting. Even when the plants are not flowering, their soft gray foliage lends interest to the garden.

How: Give mullein a well-drained soil in full sun. The plants tolerate drought and seashore conditions but won't tolerate a wet soil. In the fall, cut back the plants to neaten up appearance.

Trowels: 🌱 🌱

Veronica

Spike speedwell, veronica

Zones: 3–10

Height: *V. incana*, 12 inches; *V. spicata*, 15 inches

Sun: Full sun

Veronica spicata
'Blue Charm'

What: Veronicas are superb, long-blooming plants in wonderful shades of blue and lavender. Spike speedwell (*V. spicata*) has spikes of white, blue, or pink flowers in summer. *V. spicata* 'Sunnyborder Blue' is compact with dark violet flowers. Woolly speedwell (*V. incana*) grows to just 1 foot and forms neat clumps of silvery gray foliage. Veronicas are also wonderfully unappealing to the deer population.

Where: Use the smaller forms of veronica, such as *V. incana,* in the front of the border as edging and taller forms in the middle of the border.

How: Plant speedwell in an average soil. Deadhead plants for more flowers, and cut back or pinch back if they look floppy. The plants may sprawl untidily when the soil is too rich. Speedwell is seashore tolerant. Divide every few years for more stock.

Trowels: 🌱 🌱

Viola odorata

Sweet violet

Zones: 6–10

Height: 8–12 inches

Sun: Partial shade

What: The *Viola* genus is very big and includes popular annuals, biennials, and perennials. Sweet violets have very fragrant violet, white, or rose flowers that appear faithfully each spring. The foliage is dark green.

Where: Sweet violets are the perfect plants for a woodland or shade garden. Let them edge shady pathways.

How: Sweet violets can be planted in the spring or fall in a rich, moist soil. They benefit from an application of bonemeal very early each spring. Simply sprinkle a handful around plants and lightly rake in.

Viola odorata

Trowels: 🌱 🌱

Yucca filamentosa

Adam's-needle, yucca
Zones: 4–10
Height: 4–6 feet
Sun: Full sun

What: Yucca plants are tropical looking yet very hardy, with long, sword-like leaves and giant 6-foot plumes of cream-colored flowers in late summer. The flowers are fragrant in the evenings. Yuccas are grown more often for their foliage than for their flowers, as they add a very strong architectural element to the garden. Several colorful variegated forms exist.

Yucca filamentosa

Where: Use yuccas as accent plants for their sculptural foliage in any garden design. They look wonderful with purple flowers. They also look great in a rock garden, where they grow well and add interesting contrast to the lower-growing plants.

How: Give yucca plants a place in the sun with well-drained soil. They tolerate a wide range of difficult situations: drought, heat, humidity, seashore. In mild climates, they will grow to a large size. The foliage is evergreen; it won't die back in winter. Don't expect flowers every year; they tend to flower every couple of years. It's best to plant them in spring and not to move them. Low maintenance.

Trowels: ✐

USDA Plant Hardiness Zone Map

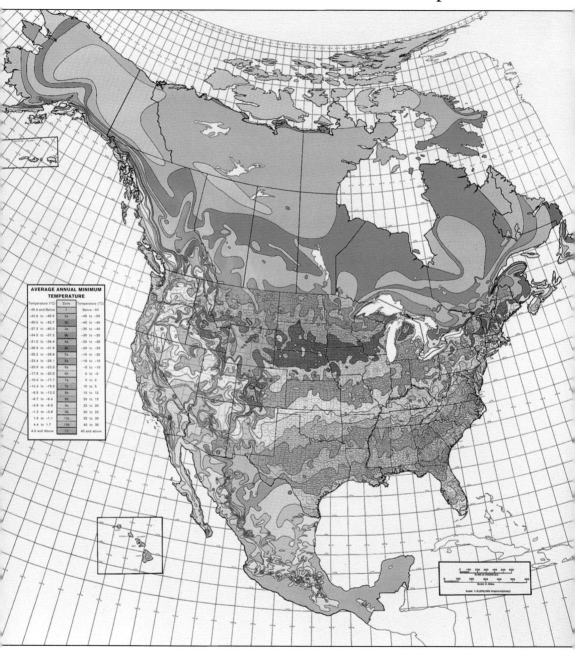

AVERAGE ANNUAL MINIMUM TEMPERATURE

Temperature (°C)	Zone	Temperature (°C)
-45.6 and Below	1	Below -50
-42.8 to -45.5	2a	-45 to -50
-40.0 to -42.7	2b	-40 to -45
-37.3 to -40.0	3a	-35 to -40
-34.5 to -37.2	3b	-30 to -35
-31.0 to -34.4	4a	-25 to -30
-28.9 to -31.6	4b	-20 to -25
-26.2 to -28.8	5a	-15 to -20
-23.4 to -26.1	5b	-10 to -15
-20.6 to -23.3	6a	-5 to -10
-17.8 to -20.5	6b	0 to -5
-15.0 to -17.7	7a	5 to 0
-12.3 to -15.0	7b	10 to 5
-9.5 to -12.2	8a	15 to 10
-6.7 to -9.4	8b	20 to 15
-3.9 to -6.6	9a	25 to 20
-1.2 to -3.8	9b	30 to 25
1.6 to -1.1	10a	35 to 30
4.4 to 1.7	10b	40 to 35
4.5 and Above	11	40 and above

The Gardener's Calendar

Use the USDA Hardiness Zone Map on the facing page to find where you are, then use the following calendar of chores to schedule your maintenance tasks throughout the year.

Zones 2–4

Early Spring

- Order bare-root perennials from mail-order nurseries.
- Begin to remove evergreen boughs as the weather warms.
- Put peony stakes in the garden.
- Have the soil tested if it hasn't done in the last three years.

Late Spring

- Clean up beds and borders.
- Plant perennials.
- Dig and divide established perennials.
- Thin phlox.
- Watch for pests—it's easier to control them if caught early.
- Pot up containers.
- Begin weeding on a regular basis.
- Stake lilies.

Summer

- Put mulches in place in garden beds.
- Perform basic garden tasks: weed, water, feed.
- Start pinching mums and asters.
- Cut flowers all summer to enjoy indoors.
- Water and feed plants in containers regularly.
- Stake plants as they need it.
- Deadhead coreopsis, geraniums, and other perennials for a second flush of flowers.

Early Autumn

- Divide daylilies and irises.
- After first hard frost, cut back perennials. Don't cut the plants with ornamental seed heads that provide winter interest.
- Plant bearded irises, peonies, and poppies.
- Move perennials in containers to a sheltered space outdoors.
- Begin raking leaves.

Late Autumn

- Rake the last of the leaves; shred and add them to the leaf mold pile to use next spring as a mulch.
- Clean and store garden tools.
- Take down and store stakes for use next year.
- Cover heavy containers that will stay outdoors with boards and a tarp.

Winter

- Add evergreen boughs as winter mulch to garden beds.
- Peruse garden catalogs.
- Walk around your property and plan new garden beds.
- Order new plants.

Zones 5–7

Early Spring

- Order bare-root perennials from mail-order nurseries.
- Begin to remove evergreen boughs from the garden . . . gradually!
- Put peony rings in place.
- Oil and sharpen tools.
- Begin weeding.
- Have the soil tested if it hasn't been done in the last three years.
- Watch for pests—hand pick aphids as you find them.

Late Spring

- Pot up containers, adding trellises for vines.
- Weed on a regular basis.
- Deadhead perennials.
- Begin to pinch back mums and asters.
- Divide fall-blooming perennials and those that have already flowered.
- Water when rainfall is scarce.

Summer

- Incorporate organic matter into the garden beds.
- Add mulches to the beds.
- Deadhead regularly.
- Perform basic garden tasks: weed, water, feed, mulch, deadhead.
- Cut flowers to enjoy indoors.
- Water and feed plants in containers regularly.
- Stake plants as they need it.

Early Autumn

- Divide daylilies and irises.
- Plant poppies, bearded irises, and peonies early.
- Dig and prepare new perennial beds.
- Begin fall cleanup: remove fallen leaves from beds, cut back perennials.
- Water all plants if rainfall is inadequate.

Late Autumn

- Compost leaves.
- Cut back perennials to 4 to 6 inches from the ground.
- Water if rain is not forecasted.

Winter

- Add evergreen boughs to beds.
- Peruse garden catalogs. Begin making a list of perennials to order.
- Plan new gardens on paper.

Zones 8–10

Early Spring

- Deadhead faded flowers to keep them blooming.
- Spread mulch in the garden beds.
- Watch for insect and disease problems.
- Turn the compost pile as needed.
- Have the soil tested if it hasn't been done in the last three years.
- Dig and divide established summer- and fall-blooming perennials.
- Consider installing a soaker hose or other drip irrigation system for the garden.

Late Spring

- Fertilize the perennials.
- Feed and water plants in containers.
- Put stakes in place.

- Water all plants when needed to prevent stress.
- Be on the lookout for aphids; hand pick them if spotted.
- Pinch back mums and asters.

Summer

- Watch for insects—especially spider mites.
- Weed.
- Cut back plants as needed to rejuvenate.
- Continue deadheading throughout summer.
- Protect newly planted perennials from excessive heat with a shade cloth.
- Stop pinching mums and asters.

Early Autumn

- Water and feed annuals.
- Deadhead frequently.
- Check the containers often to see if the soil is dry.
- Weed regularly.

Late Autumn

- Cut the perennials back to 4–6 inches.
- Remove debris from the flower beds.
- Harvest flowers for drying.
- Continue monitoring the garden for pests and diseases.
- Water as necessary.
- Stake plants as necessary.
- Mulch the garden bed.

Winter

- Water as needed when temperatures are above freezing.
- Deadhead as necessary.
- Remove fall garden debris, till the soil deeply, and incorporate organic matter.
- Renew the mulches.
- Look through seed catalogs for new plants.
- Clean and sharpen garden tools.

Spacing
Perennials

Here are the recommended spacing distances for perennials. Remember that perennials need two to three years to reach their full size and width.

Achillea spp. (yarrow), $1^1/_2$ feet
A. filipendulina (fern-leaf yarrow), 2 feet
Aconitum carmichaelii (azure monkshood), 2 feet
Agapanthus africanus (agapanthus), 2 feet
Alchemilla mollis (lady's-mantle), $1^1/_2$ feet
Amsonia tabernaemontana (bluestar), 2–3 feet
Anemone × *hybrida* (Japanese anemone), 2 feet
Aquilegia hybrids (columbine), $1^1/_2$ feet
Artemisia ludoviciana (wormwood), 2–3 feet

A. schmidtiana (wormwood), $1^1/_2$ feet

Aruncus dioicus (goatsbeard), 3 feet

Asclepias tuberosa (butterfly weed), $1^1/_2$ feet

Aster × *frikartii* (Frikart's aster), $1^1/_2$ feet

Astilbe × *arendsii* (astilbe), $1^1/_2$–$2^1/_2$ feet

Aurinia saxatilis (basket-of-gold, goldentuft), 1 foot

Baptisia australis (blue false indigo), 3 feet

Boltonia asteroides (boltonia), 2–4 feet

Brunnera macrophylla (Siberian bugloss), 2 feet

Campanula carpatica (Carpathian bellflower), $1^1/_2$ feet

C. lactifolia (milky bellflower), 2 feet

C. persicifolia (peach-leafed bellflower), 1–$1^1/_2$ feet

Canna × *generalis* (canna), $1^1/_2$–3 feet

Cerastium tomentosum (snow-in-summer), 2 feet

Ceratostigma plumbaginoides (plumbago, leadwort), $1^1/_2$ feet

Cimicifuga racemosa (bugbane, black snakeroot), 2 feet

Convallaria majalis (lily-of-the-valley), 1 foot

Coreopsis verticillata (threadleaf coreopsis), 2 feet

Crambe cordifolia (colewort, giant kale), 3 feet

Dendranthema × *grandiflorum* (garden mum), $1^1/_2$ feet

Dianthus plumarius (cottage pink), 8 inches

Dicentra eximia (fringed bleeding-heart) 1–$1^1/_2$ feet

D. spectabilis (bleeding-heart), $1^1/_2$ feet

Digitalis × *mertonensis* (foxglove), 1 foot

Echinacea purpurea (purple coneflower), $1^1/_2$–2 feet

Echinops ritro (globe thistle), $1^1/_2$ feet

Gaillardia × *grandiflora* (blanketflower), $1^1/_2$ feet

Geranium spp. (cranesbill, hardy geraniums), $1^1/_2$–2 feet

Gypsophila paniculata (baby's breath), 4 feet

Helenium autumnale (sneezeweed), $1^1/_2$ feet

Heliopsis helianthoides (false sunflower), 2 feet

Hemerocallis × *hybrida* (daylily), 2–3 feet

Heuchera spp. and hybrids (heuchera), 1 foot

Hosta fortunei (hosta), 2 feet

H. sieboldiana (hosta), $2^1/_2$–4 feet

H. undulata (wavy-leaf plantain lily), 1–$1^1/_2$ feet

Iris, bearded, 1–2 feet

Iris ensata (Japanese iris), $1^1/_2$ feet

I. pseudacorus (yellow flag), $1^1/_2$ feet

I. sibirica (Siberian iris), 3 feet

Lavandula angustifolia (English lavender), 2–3 feet

Leucanthemum × *superbum* (Shasta daisy), $1^1/_2$–2 feet

Liatris spicata (spike gayfeather), $1^1/_2$ feet

Liriope muscari (lilyturf), $1^1/_2$ feet

Lobelia cardinalis (cardinal flower), 1 foot

L. siphilitica (great blue lobelia), 1 foot

L. × *speciosa* (lobelia), 2 feet

Lysimachia clethroides (gooseneck loosestrife), 3 feet

L. nummularia (creeping Jenny), 6–8 inches

Malva alcea (hollyhock mallow), 1 feet

M. moschata (musk mallow), 2 feet

Monarda didyma (bee balm), $1^1/_2$ feet

Myosotis scorpioides (forget-me-not), 2 feet

Nepeta mussinii (catmint), 1 foot

Nipponanthemum nipponicum (Nippon daisy, Montauk daisy), 2 feet

Oenothera missouriensis (Missouri primrose), 2 feet

O. tetragona (sundrops), 1 foot

Paeonia lactiflora (peony), 2–3 feet

Papaver orientale (oriental poppy), 2–3 feet

Penstemon digitalis (beardtongue), 2–3 feet

Perovskia atriplicifolia (Russian sage), $1^1/_2$–2 feet

Phlox paniculata (border phlox), 2 feet

Physostegia virginia (obedient plant), $1^1/_2$ feet

Platycodon grandiflorus (balloonflower), 1 foot

Polygonatum odoratum (Solomon's seal), 1 foot

Primula japonica (Japanese primrose), 1 foot

P. × *polyantha* (polyanthus primrose), 9 feet

Rudbeckia fulgida (black-eyed Susan), $1^1/_2$ feet

Salvia × *superba* (meadow sage), $1^1/_2$ feet

Scabiosa caucasica (pincushion flower), 1 foot

Sedum 'Autumn Joy' (sedum), $1^1/_2$ feet

S. 'Ruby Glow' (sedum), 1 foot

S. spectabile (showy stonecrop), $1^1/_2$–2 feet

Sempervivum tectorum (hens and chickens), 1 foot

Sidalcea malviflora (prairie mallow), 1 foot

Solidago hybrids (goldenrod), $1^1/_2$–2 feet

Stachys byzantina (lamb's ears), 1 foot

Stokesia laevis (Stoke's aster), 1 foot

Tanacetum parthenium (feverfew), 1 foot

Tradescantia virginiana (spiderwort), 2 feet

Verbascum × *hybridum* (mullein), $1^1/_2$ feet

Veronica incana (woolly speedwell), $1^1/_2$ feet

V. spicata (spike speedwell), 1 foot

Viola odorata (sweet violet), 1 foot

Yucca filamentosa (Adam's-needle), 2–3 feet

The Gardener's Language

Accents   Single plants used in a garden design. Accent plants tend to have strong characteristics, such as dramatic or interesting foliage.

Acidic soil   Soil with a pH value of less than 7.0.

Alkaline soil   Soil with a pH value of more than 7.0.

Annuals   Plants that live for one year or growing season.

Bare root   Perennials that are sold in their dormant stage with all soil removed from the roots. Many plants are shipped from mail-order nurseries bare root and packed in a lightweight shipping material.

Beneficial insects   Insects, such as ladybugs, lacewings, dragonflies, and certain wasps and flies, that eat or parasitize the insects that damage plants.

Biennials   Plants that take two years to complete their life cycles; they germinate the first year, and flower the second.

Broadcast To scatter seeds or fertilizer onto the soil by hand.

Bud A flower bud develops into a flower; a growth bud on the tip of a stem or along the side of a stem will produce new leafy growth.

Clay soil A type of soil with small, almost microscopic soil particles.

Complete fertilizer A plant food, either organic or synthetic, with all three of the essential nutrient elements: nitrogen, phosphorus, and potassium.

Compost Decomposed organic matter that is added to the soil to improve its composition and fertility.

Crown The part of a plant between the stem and root, where the two sections join.

Cultivar A plant variety that is selected from cultivation, not from the wild. When propagated, it retains its distinct identity.

Cultivate The act of tilling or stirring the soil surface to eliminate weeds and aerate the soil.

Cutting The piece of a plant, usually a stem, cut off from the plant and rooted to make a new plant.

Deadhead The act of removing faded flowers to promote further flowering, prevent seeding, or improve the appearance of a plant.

Disbud To remove emerging flower buds to encourage the plant to produce bigger flowers.

Direct sow The act of planting seeds directly in the soil where they are to grow.

Diseases Organisms (fungal, viral, or bacterial) that attack plants, hindering their development and producing mildews, rots, rusts, and wilts on stems, leaves, and flowers.

Divide A way of propagating perennials by separating into two or more pieces to reinvigorate the plants.

Dormancy The period during which a plant stops showing signs of growth. Perennials are dormant in the winter.

Evergreen A plant or tree that never loses all its leaves at the same time.

Family   A biological division within the plant or animal kingdom that comprises genera. *See also* **Genus**.

Fertilizer   Any material, synthetic or organic, that supplies nutrients to a plant.

Foliage plants   Plants used in gardens primarily for their attractive foliage rather than for flowers.

Formal   A rigid geometric garden design that incorporates plants that have neat and tidy shapes.

Genus   A division of organisms within a family. It may contain one or more species. *See also* **Species**.

Ground cover   A low-growing plant that forms a mat of foliage.

Harden off   The process of introducing a plant to outdoor temperatures by gradually acclimating it to colder weather, minimizing the shock of the transition.

Hardiness zone   The climate in which a perennial is deemed hardy based on the plant's ability to tolerate the climatic conditions within a particular geographical area. The USDA Plant Hardiness Zone Map divides North America into eleven hardiness zones.

Heavy soil   Used interchangeably with *clay soil* to describe a soil made up of minutely fine particles packed close together.

Herbaceous   Perennials with nonwoody stems. Refers to plants that die back each winter and produce new stems the following growing season.

Humus   Organic matter in its last stage of decay, usually brown or black.

Hybrid   A plant that has been created by cross-pollinating different plants to create a new plant that is distinct from or superior to its parents.

Inflorescence   The flower-supporting structure of plants: umbels, corymbs, spikes, and racemes.

Informal   A free-form garden design that incorporates plants that often drift and sprawl into each other and spill over the sides of the garden.

Invasive   A plant that spreads quickly and, if not checked, can take over a garden.

Island bed   A garden bed that is set within a lawn. Its shape may be geometric or free-form.

Leaf mold   Leaves that have decomposed and can be dug into the soil as an organic amendment.

Loam   A balance of sand and clay; the best type of soil.

Manure   Livestock dung, usually high in nutrients, used as an organic fertilizer and soil conditioner.

Microclimate   An area with either colder or warmer temperatures than those around it, usually owing to the existence of a wall, large body of water, slope, streets, or buildings.

Mulch   Materials, synthetic or organic, spread on the soil surface to protect plants from excessive weather, stifle the growth of weeds, conserve moisture, or to enhance the look of a garden.

Native plant   A plant that is naturally found in a particular region. Plants are easiest to grow in their native habitat, because they are adapted to that particular environment.

Naturalize   To plant out randomly in a way that imitates nature and makes it appear as though the plants grew there naturally. Some plants will naturalize once planted, meaning they will continue to spread or reseed themselves.

Neutral soil   Soil that is neither too alkaline nor too acid, it has a pH value of 7.0. The broadest spectrum of nutrients reach plants in soils with a neutral pH.

Nitrogen   One of the three most important nutrients for a plant. Nitrogen helps plants produce stems and leaves.

Organic matter   Any material that was once alive or that came from a living creature: compost, sawdust, and fish emulsion are examples.

Perennials   Plants whose life cycles take more than two years to complete.

Pests   The range of insects and animals that attack and damage plants, including aphids, mites, slugs, birds, rabbits, and deer.

pH A measure of acidity on a scale of 0 to 14. The lowest end of the scale is the most acidic, the highest is most alkaline, and the middle (7.0) is neutral.

Phosphorus One of the three most important nutrients for a plant. It helps plants develop flowers, seeds, and roots.

Pinching A process of pruning (with forefingers or scissors) to keep plants growing compactly and encourage bushiness.

Potassium One of the three most important nutrients for a plant. Potassium helps the plant grow and develop strong stems.

Potbound The condition of a container-grown plant whose root ball is thickly matted.

Root ball The entire root system of a plant in soil.

Runner A stem that spreads horizontally through the soil sending out roots at various points. Many weeds grow by runners.

Sandy soil A type of soil that has large soil particles.

Self-sowing Plants that sow their own seeds into the ground.

Slug An invertebrate mammal in the mollusk family that often hides under stones and boards, feeding on leaves in the night. Slug damage is manifest by the chewed leaves.

Soil test An analysis of the soil to determine its pH level and the nutrients available.

Species A division of organisms within a genus.

Stake A structure to support plants that may otherwise flop over.

Succulent A plant with juicy, water-storing stems or leaves.

Taproot The main root of a plant that grows directly downward.

Till To cultivate the soil.

Transplant A newly moved plant; the act of moving a plant from one location to another.

Variety Plants within a species that are slightly different from other members of that species.

Variegated foliage   Foliage that has more than one color, usually white or yellow in spots, ribbons, or other identifiable pattern.

Vermiculite   A mica-type rock expanded by heat that is lightweight and absorbent; is used in seed-starting and growing media.

Volunteer   Seedling from a plant that sowed its own seeds into the garden.

Weed   An unwanted plant in the garden. Eliminating weeds improves the appearance of a garden and provides growing space for plants that are wanted.

Index

Page numbers in *italics* indicate photographs or illustrations.